WOODLAND DRUMMER
RUFFED GROUSE

598.635
Fur

National Wildlife Federation® is the nation's largest conservation, education and advocacy organization. Since 1936, NWF has educated people from all walks of life to protect nature, wildlife and the world we all share.

For more information about National Wildlife Federation, write: National Wildlife Federation, 8925 Leesburg Pike, Vienna, Virginia 22184.

NWF's World Wide Web Site www.nwf.org provides instant computer access to information about National Wildlife Federation, conservation issues and ideas for getting involved in protecting our world.

©National Wildlife Federation, 1999 ™ and ® designate trademarks of National Wildlife Federation and are used, under license, by Creative Publishing international, Inc.

NorthWord Press
5900 Green Oak Drive
Minnetonka, MN 55343
1-800-328-3895

Library of Congress Cataloging-in-Publication Data
Furtman, Michael
　　Ruffed grouse : woodland drummer / Michael Furtman.
　　　　p. cm.
　　Includes bibliographical references (p.　) and index.
　　ISBN 1-55971-714-9
　　1. Ruffed grouse.　I. Title.
QL696.G285F87　1999
598.6'35—dc21　　　　　　　　　　　　99-14992

Printed in Malaysia

WOODLAND DRUMMER
RUFFED GROUSE

by Michael Furtman

NORTHWORD®
NORTHWORD PRESS
Minnetonka, Minnesota

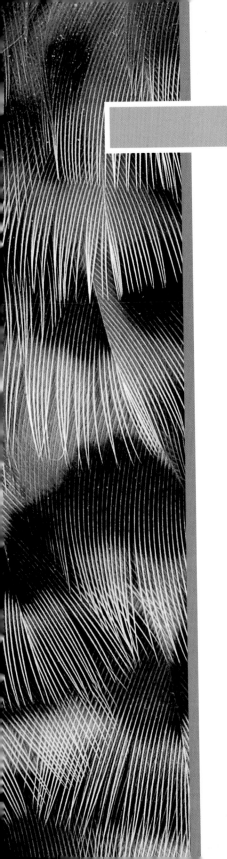

Dedication

In memory of my father,
who always made time
to take me to the woods,
and to Gypsy and Rascal,
two fine grouse dogs
fondly missed.

Table of Contents

Introduction

A WALK IN RUFFED GROUSE WOODS is a wonderful thing.

Ruffed grouse woods are lush, frequently young, and often thick. Life in them percolates at a rapid rate and yet, because of the denseness of the forest, its occupants are often hidden from our sight.

And it makes no difference whether you walk those grouse woods in the dampness of spring, when fern fronds curl daintily from the black soil, or in the starkness of winter, when snow silences the eternal forest. Grouse woods are good places to be.

For those of us who not only admire the secretive ruffed grouse, but also hunt it for the joy of oneness with nature and the incredible food that the ruffed grouse is, autumn is the best time to be in ruffed grouse country. The forest is ablaze with color, painted against a canvas of blue autumn skies. Brackens and ferns, brown and wilting, still hide the secretive ruffed grouse so that when one flushes—often with long walks in between—it lifts into the air in a thunderous whirring that halts the hearts of humans and quickens those of hunting dogs. It is a time cherished by many, a chance to rejoin nature however briefly, to touch however tentatively the ancient cycle of life and death. It is a time to garner spiritual and physical sustenance from the bounty of this earth.

Ruffed grouse are symbolic of vibrant, young forests.

But whenever we go to the grouse woods, or for whatever reason, we are bound to not only sense its life, but marvel at its complexity. Whereas old forests are magnificent in their stature, inspirational in their grandeur, and, unfortunately, melancholic in their rarity, young forests can also renew our spirits, serve as reminders that nature's way is one of incredible fecundity, and demonstrate the earth's spectacular ability to renew itself and all its dependent life forms. And since ruffed grouse thrive best in young to middle-aged forests, they tend to be a visible reminder of this vitality.

Ruffed grouse are also an enigma.

Most of the time, they are a shy, well-concealed forest bird seldom seen except by those specifically looking for them. Yet when we do unexpectedly encounter one, they can cause great alarm. Bursting from beneath a balsam fir or bracken ferns, they thunder off, corkscrewing their way through the tangled net of tree limbs and brush, their sudden appearance leaving us shocked.

So too can they startle us when we encounter a hen with a brood. Ruffed grouse are very protective of their young, and a hen will charge even a human, or provide us with an Academy Award performance, feigning a broken wing in an effort to lure us away from her chicks.

I've been fortunate enough to be startled frequently by grouse. It may be a strange thing to some—that I relish the momentary fright—but to me it means that I've been spending time in the grouse woods, time enough to encounter this special bird. Whether I've stumbled upon them while carrying a canoe across a portage in the wilderness, or been surprised by one while hunting in the autumn, they never cease to jump-start my cardiovascular system.

Once, on a May morning with the grass wet with dew, my father and I came across a hen with chicks. I was a young boy then, and we were on an excursion far back into the Minnesota woods, in search of wild brook trout and the sparkling, well-hidden creek that contained them. The forest was dense despite the fact that leaves were just emerging, for we were walking through an area that had been logged over a decade or more before. Young trees were everywhere and so near together that walking with a fly rod in hand was a difficult thing to do. I clearly remember cresting a small rise on the barely discernible game trail we were hiking, when suddenly a ruffed grouse whirled on the ground before us in a frantic display of near-death pain.

Of course, she was acting, convincingly dragging one limp wing as she spun and tried to lead us farther down the trail. We were stunned, confused at first, until we deciphered her ruse. Then my father smiled at me, told me that here we had a worried hen that must have a brood near-by, and urged me to be careful where I stepped. We paused and looked to our feet, and there, so marvelously camouflaged that they nearly escaped our detection, were 6 or 7 speckled chicks.

The hen continued to try to lead us away. We decided to humor her, and carefully followed her down the trail, watching where we put our feet less we crush a hidden chick. When she would get too far ahead she would stop and try to convince us once again that she was injured and catchable, then would scurry on, wing dragging, as we neared. After a

Secretive and camouflaged, ruffed grouse are rarely seen except when they startle us, or we startle them.

performance that lasted but a few minutes and that took us perhaps 30 yards, she ducked off the trail into thicker brush, then launched herself into flight at a right angle from the trail.

We watched her fly off, curving all the time to our right, probably etching an arc that would take her back to her brood. Dad and I chuckled and laughed, thrilled at this wonderful display and the miracle of nature, and then forged back down the brushy trail. There were brook trout waiting to be caught.

Minnesota is grouse country. In parts of the state, it is about as good as it gets if you're a grouse, or a grouse hunter. Much research has been done in this, my home state, on the ruffed grouse, a great deal of it near my home at the Cloquet Forestry Center, a University of Minnesota forestry research and education facility.

There are many scientists who have studied the ruffed grouse in locations across its range. The late Gordon Gullion, who did most of his famous ruffed grouse research at Cloquet, and whom I had the pleasure

Many people—researchers, hunters, and wildlife biologists—
work to keep ruffed grouse populations healthy.

to meet on several occasions, was enamored of this bird and devoted most of his professional life to unlocking the secrets of its existence. You will read his name often in this book, for he was the most prolific of researchers, penning dozens of papers and a book on ruffed grouse.

But Gullion's work, as important as it was, doesn't paint a complete picture, for ruffed grouse are found in places that don't resemble the mixed apsen-birch-fir forests of Minnesota. Many other scientists, like Dr. Gardiner Bump, whose 1930s research on ruffed grouse in New York laid seminal groundwork on the topic, have contributed to the knowledge I've distilled into this book. Among others whose research I studied and which contributed significantly to this text are Frank Thompson III, Donald Rusch, Ronald Runkles, John Kubisiak, Stephen Maxson, Stephen DeStafano, and Fred Brenner. Together, these scientists and others have probed the intricacies of this unassuming bird's life, resulting in a picture that, although still incomplete, reveals the oft-hidden life of the ruffed grouse.

That some mystery remains is not an altogether bad thing. We know very much about this valued bird, enough to help manage its habitat to ensure that it prospers. Hunters particularly play an important role in deciding its future, often working with state divisions of wildlife or through this bird's premier advocacy group, the Ruffed Grouse Society. But management and science aside, the secret nature of the ruffed grouse—and its occasional eruptions into our startled conscience—is also a mystery worth valuing.

For the life of the ruffed grouse is fraught with danger, rife with competition, and brimming with riddles. Learning how and where they live, what it is that they do, is a fascinating thing.

But we should never lose track that they do these things not for us, but for themselves, and as a part of a larger cycle that includes the hawks and owls, the foxes and bobcats, and in a forest shared with deer and woodcock and bears. That mystery, that cycle, and the ruffed grouse's role in it all, is something to cherish, something that, though we understand a few of the parts, in its complexity fills us with awe.

The forests would be a quieter place, a lesser place, diminished in excitement and beauty were there no ruffed grouse.

I, for one, am thankful they exist.

CHAPTER ONE

On the Wings of Time
Evolution and Taxonomy

IMAGINE A TIME in the planet's distant past when the world's temperature was stable and warm. Across the entire north temperate zone of North America and Eurasia, a similar forest grew, one rich in hardwoods—a lush, contiguous forest of massive proportions. The time was the Miocene epoch, 10 to 25 million years ago, and the world was beginning to look something like the one we know today. The animals and birds, though different in form from those around now, were creatures we would recognize as related to those we know today. Thanks to the warmth of the period, coastlines were submerged beneath the rising waters of melting glaciers and polar ice caps. Large grazing animals were just beginning to roam North America's newly developing grasslands, grasslands forming in the rain shadows of the Rockies as the mountains thrust up in the era's upheavals. In the great forests, large browsing mammals thrived. And in that vast forest, there were grouse.

The evolutionary path of the ruffed grouse is many millions of years long.

EVOLUTION

These grouse were not today's grouse—neither the ruffed, spruce, or blue grouse. These grouse were an earlier form, an unknown ancestor, but one whose descendants would evolve into the grouse with which we are familiar. The earliest known North American fossil grouse, *Paleoalectoris incertus*, dates to the beginning of the Miocene, about 25 million years ago. Although it is from a genus with no surviving offshoots, it indicates that grouse were not only already present, but well evolved. Soon after—in the long look of geologic time—another grouse for which we have fossils appeared, *Tympanuchus stirtoni,* about 10 million years ago. The relationship of these early grouse to our ruffed grouse is unclear.

Because birds have hollow, delicate bones that are easily destroyed by the actions of the earth and by weather, the fossil record of the grouse's evolution is, and probably will remain, incomplete. However, it is believed that the wide array of grouse we know today evolved from the birds of the closely related pheasant family. As they evolved, they lost the attributes of the warm-climate pheasants—sharp tarsal spurs, long tails, and iridescent plumage—and gained the features that distinguish cool-climate grouse—feathers that cover the lower legs and the nostrils, which are adaptations for colder weather.

These adaptations were necessary during the cooler, drier Pliocene epoch, which followed the Miocene. As the North American continent took shape, as temperatures changed, and as the forests began to evolve away from the contiguous hardwoods to a more diverse melange, grouse evolved to fill these new niches. Similar events were occurring across Europe and Asia. Tundra appeared, grasslands expanded, and vast conifer forests grew. Each of these environments offered new challenges and benefits to grouse-like birds. Most of the habitats that were created then exist yet today, as do a number of the species that evolved during that period. Whatever ancestor it was that became the ruffed grouse, it has had over 10 million years to perfect the form and behavior we see today.

TAXONOMY

Scientists classify life forms using a system first developed in the 1750s by Carolus Linnaeus, a professor at Sweden's University of Uppsala. According to this system, the ruffed grouse falls in the order Galliformes (chicken-like birds), which itself is broken down into families, such as Numidinae (African guinea fowl), or Phasianidae, the family in which grouse, pheasants, quail, and partridges are found.

The family Phasianidae is further broken down into subfamilies, like Phasianini, which contains the true Old World pheasants characterized by their long tails, bright plumage, and sharp tarsal spurs. Grouse are in their own and separate subfamily, Tetraoninae, which contains fourteen species in total divided into six *genera* (genus). Ruffed grouse are in the genus Bonasa, along with two closely related Eurasian grouse. The other familiar grouse of North America are in different genera: the spruce and blue grouse, both adapted to conifer forests, are respectively classified as *Dendragapus canadensis* and *Dendragapus obscuris.*

A needle-eating grouse, the spruce grouse's range overlaps the ruffed grouse's in the northern boreal forest.

The blue grouse inhabits the conifer forests of the Rocky Mountains.

The sharp-tailed grouse and pinnated grouse (prairie chicken)—close relatives to each other and dwellers of grasslands—are in another genus and are classified as *Tympanuchus phasianellus* and *Tympanuchus cupido.* Finally, the grouse of the tundra, the ptarmigan, are in the genus *Lagopus,* one member of which dwells in North America, *L. leucurus.*

Zoologists and taxonomists spend a great deal of time classifying birds and animals, although to most of us such efforts seem a bit extreme. But for the lay person, this hierarchy can be helpful, because even to our untrained eyes, grouse, pheasants, quail, and the barnyard chicken clearly are related. As we trace back up this family tree—from a specific like the ruffed grouse to the general, such as its family, we are most likely also tracing its evolution. Each of these species sprouted from some earlier ancestor. Each evolved to fit specific niches in the ecosystem. The further back we go in time, and the further toward the roots of the family tree we go, the simpler the system, and the less evolved, and probably less specialized, was the progenitor.

The sharp-tailed grouse has evolved to live in grassland and brushland habitats.

WHAT'S IN A NAME?

In addition to being classified in an Order and Family, each species is given a specific Latin name. In the case of the ruffed grouse, it is *Bonasa umbellus*—a mouthful, perhaps, for such a quiet and unassuming bird, but one that fits it to a T.

Ruffed grouse have frequently been called the "drummer in the woods," named for the sound the male makes when trying to attract a mate or defend its territory. To many people today, the drumming sound the ruffed grouse makes is similar to a small two-cycle motor starting up. But when ruffed grouse were named, there were no internal combustion motors. Yet the first half of its Latin name relates to its drumming sound. So what does "bonasa" mean? It derives from the root word for "bison"—the buffalo of North America. And it suggests that the drumming of the grouse sounds like the thundering of hooves, or at least it did to the person who gave the ruffed grouse its Latin name.

Ptarmigan are the most northerly dwelling members of the grouse family.

Overleaf: The sound made by the male ruffed grouse—called drumming—travels well in the dense young forests it calls home.

The second half of its name—"umbellus"—describes a physical feature of the ruffed grouse, the one feature common to both its everyday name and its scientific classification. That feature is its "ruff," the collar of specialized feathers around its neck. This ruff of neck feathers, which is fluffed up in display, appears to be nearly black, but on close inspection reveals tones of iridescent violet or dark blue. And so "umbellus" reveals the bird's ability to open its "umbrella" of erect feathers.

A more literal, and silly sounding, translation of the Latin *Bonasa umbellus* might be "bison umbrella" or "thundering umbrella." It is just as well then that we stick with its common name, the ruffed grouse.

Of course, not everyone uses even that common name. Across its range in North America, which is larger than that of any other North American grouse, the ruffed grouse is known by a few colloquial names, the most frequent of which is "partridge." It is also the most inaccurate, for there really are true partridges, and the ruffed grouse, though distantly related, is not a part of that group. Partridges are natives of the Old World and are seed eaters that do best in fairly warm, dry climates. Grouse are more northerly birds, well adapted to surviving the rigors of both cold and snow, and eat buds and flowers.

CLOSE RELATIVES

In fact, it is this adaptation to cooler temperatures that largely makes a grouse a grouse. In order to take advantage of the many cool-climate niches that were being created by changing global climate patterns, grouse developed feathered legs to help ward off the cold. And although the beak of a grouse looks shorter than that of similarly sized members of the pheasant family, this shortness is really just an illusion. All grouse have feathers that extend down their beak to cover their nostrils, which helps to slow and warm icy air before it is inhaled, but which makes the beak look short. The degree to which these features are noticeable depends upon the species of grouse. They are most noticeable on the tundra-dwelling ptarmigans, which endure cold far greater, and longer in duration, than do ruffed grouse.

Note the feathers on this grouse's lower legs and beak—both of which are adaptations for surviving cold weather.

Nature abhors a vacuum. And so, as the ancestral grouse of those ancient forests encountered the newer, cooler, drier environments of the Pliocene, succeeding generations became more and more specialized to utilize these ecological niches. The forest-dwelling ancestors of today's prairie grouse—sharp-tailed grouse and prairie chicken—moved onto the newly forming savannas and grasslands. Another offshoot evolved on the tundra and became the ptarmigan. Since vast conifer forests were now growing on mountainsides and in the North, it would make sense that needle-eating grouse would evolve. They did, and today we have two North American species, the spruce and the blue grouse.

One might assume that the ruffed grouse's nearest relative would be these other grouse species—the blue and spruce grouse—that share or overlap parts of its range. That is not the case, however, and we must look across the Atlantic and Pacific oceans to find other members of the genus *Bonasa*. As the ruffed grouse was evolving in North America, similar evolutionary factors must have been underway in Eurasia. For that is where the ruffed grouse's nearest relative is found: two species of hazel grouse. *Bonasa bonasia* can be found in Europe from France to Scandinavia, and eastward as far as Japan. *Bonasa sewerzowi* lives in western China's mountains. Both species of hazel grouse inhabit forests very similar to those preferred by our ruffed grouse, and their life habits and habitat choices parallel those of the ruffed grouse.

For if the spruce grouse prefers the conifer forests, and the sharp-tailed grouse the prairie, the ruffed grouse found its own ecological niche, one of early successional deciduous forests. That is, they do best in the early stages of mixed north temperate forests, a forest in which conifers are present, but not dominant. In the northern part of the ruffed grouse's range, conifers are the climax, or final, stage of forest succession. Ruffed grouse prefer the aspen-birch-fir community, which is a widespread component in the boreal forest wherever fire or disease (and, today, logging) causes forest disturbance and renewal. Aspen is a major component of this successional stage, and the ruffed grouse's range correlates closely to the range of aspen forests. In these forests, ruffed grouse feed extensively on the leaves, catkins, and buds of aspen and related trees, although many hundreds of other items find their way into their diet.

Where ruffed grouse are found elsewhere, such as in the West or Pacific Northwest, they find a niche in the sub-climax deciduous forests, which also are a stage in the progression to these regions' pine-fir climax forests. Frequently, willows and cottonwoods serve as substitutes for aspen in some regions, while oak-hickory forests serve in others.

SUBSPECIES

There is a distinction between a subspecies and a species, and the rule is pretty simple: animals of two different species, although in the same family of animals, cannot produce fertile offspring when they mate. Animals of different subspecies within a species can. Thus, pheasants and grouse can't produce viable offspring together, but two ruffed grouse from different subspecies could.

And indeed, there are different subspecies of ruffed grouse across North America—twelve in all—differentiated primarily by their coloration and geographic location. Ruffed grouse come in two color phases—gray and brown (or red), with many "split-phase" individuals that are various blends of the two dominant colors. Both phases can exist in one region, but usually one color phase predominates. Each subspecies is keenly adapted to its local environment. So, the first taxonomic name of an animal is its genus, the second name, its species, and the third name, its subspecies.

The pinnated grouse, or prairie chicken, is a grassland dweller.

Eastern Ruffed Grouse *(Bonasa umbellus umbellus)*
The fact that its second and third names are the same indicates that this subspecies is the "standard" or nominate subspecies. Brown phase birds usually outnumber gray phase in this subspecies, which is found in eastern Pennsylvania and eastern Long Island, New Jersey, Rhode Island, and from western Connecticut through central New York and southern Massachusetts.

St. Lawrence Ruffed Grouse *(B.u. togata)*
Somewhat larger than the nominate subspecies, this predominately gray phase ruffed grouse has a broad range the length of the St. Lawrence River and Great Lakes. It is also known as the Canada ruffed grouse. The western end of its range is in northeastern Minnesota and it follows the transition between the northern boreal forest and the eastern deciduous forest east across northern Wisconsin, Michigan, most of New York, New Hampshire, Vermont, Maine, and Nova Scotia on the south side of the Great Lakes and St. Lawrence River. It also ranges north of these water bodies in southern Ontario from the Manitoba border east through southern Quebec.

Appalachian Ruffed Grouse *(B.u. monticola)*
Living in the eastern deciduous forests, this ruffed grouse subspecies ranges from southeastern Michigan and the north shores of Lake Ontario in Ontario, south through the western four-fifths of Pennsylvania, eastern Ohio, West Virginia, mountainous parts of Maryland, eastern Kentucky, and the highlands of Virginia, eastern Tennessee, and western North and South Carolina. The dominant color phase is brown.

Midwestern Ruffed Grouse *(B.u. mediana)*
Similar in color to the eastern ruffed grouse, with which it was lumped until 1957, it is now identified as a separate subspecies largely because of its geographic isolation. It thrives in the oak-hickory ecosystems, from east central Minnesota, south through southern Wisconsin, a sliver of

northwestern Illinois, and parts of southern Michigan, northwestern Ohio, and parts of Indiana. Missouri's ruffed grouse reintroduction program used this subspecies when releasing birds in the north central and Missouri River regions.

Gray Ruffed Grouse *(B.u. umbelloides)*
With the largest range of any of the subspecies, this bird dwells in a broad swath from extreme southeastern Alaska, British Columbia, and across the northern coniferous forests of Alberta, Manitoba, Ontario, Quebec, and southeastern Labrador. In the United States, outside Alaska, it is found only in western Montana, southeastern Idaho, and northwestern Wyoming. Although its name implies it is a gray ruffed grouse, the brown color phase does exist.

Yukon Ruffed Grouse *(B.u. yukonensis)*
The northernmost of the subspecies, this ruffed grouse is found primarily in interior Alaska, the Yukon, and Northwest Territories, dipping slightly into extreme northern Alberta and Saskatchewan. It is the largest of the ruffed grouse, with the greatest degree of feathering on its legs, and is principally a gray color phase subspecies.

Hoary Ruffed Grouse *(B.u. incana)*
The range of this subspecies is extremely disjointed. Found in a swath of habitat across the aspen parklands of the prairie provinces of Manitoba and Saskatchewan, as well as the Turtle Mountains of north central North Dakota, a distinct population lives far away to the southwest in southeastern Idaho and adjacent western Wyoming, parts of Utah, and western South Dakota. It derives its "hoary" name from its tendency to grow gray with age.

Idaho Ruffed Grouse *(B.u. phaia)*
The range of this gray phase ruffed grouse includes most of the northern two-thirds of Idaho, with small overlaps into extreme eastern Oregon and far northeastern Washington.

Olympic Ruffed Grouse *(B.u. castanea)*
Inhabiting the damp coastal forests of far western Oregon and Washington, this ruffed grouse is chestnut colored, for which no gray phase is known to exist.

Vancouver Ruffed Grouse *(B.u. brunnescens)*
Inhabiting moist coniferous forest similar to that inhabited by the nearby Olympic subspecies, the Vancouver ruffed grouse dwells on the island of the same name, as well as on portions of the British Columbia mainland adjacent to the island. It is a prevailingly gray phase subspecies.

Pacific Ruffed Grouse *(B.u. sabini)*
Inhabiting drier portions of the Pacific Northwest rain forests than either the Olympic or Vancouver subspecies, the Pacific ruffed grouse has a range lying immediately to their east, on the west side of the Cascade Mountains. This range begins in extreme northern California in the south, runs through western Oregon and western Washington, and ends in extreme southern British Columbia in the north. Brown phase birds predominate.

Columbian Ruffed Grouse *(B.u. affinis)*
Living on the eastern side of the Cascade Mountains, this primarily gray phased ruffed grouse was once considered to be the same subspecies as the Gray ruffed grouse *(B.u. umbelloides)*. It exists in central and eastern Oregon, north through eastern Washington and into south central British Columbia.

This then is the ruffed grouse: dweller of young forests, linked inexorably across much of its range to trees of the aspen family. And as simple as it sounds, the ruffed grouse's relationship with this forest and the other creatures that dwell there is both complicated and fascinating.

Although it is unlikely we'll ever fully understand the marvelous complexity of the ruffed grouse's evolution, its path to where it stands today is many tens of millions of years long. Thanks to the tests of climate and habitat, we have the ruffed grouse.

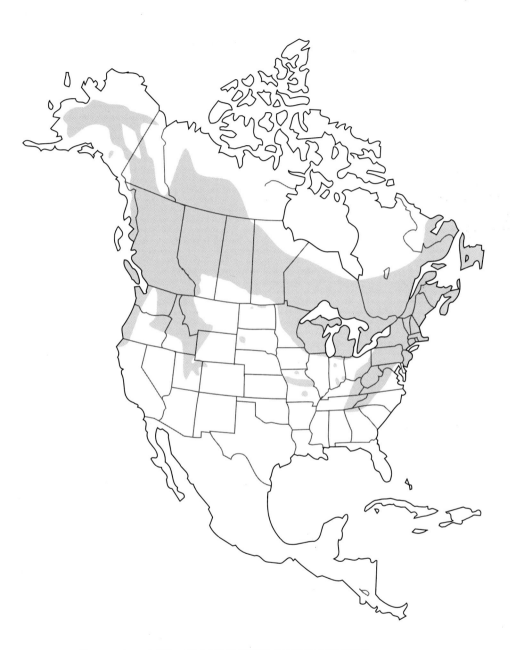

The current range of the ruffed grouse in North America is indeed large.

CHAPTER TWO

A Bird in Hand
Habitat and Physical Description

NO GROUSE IN NORTH AMERICA has as large a range as does the ruffed grouse. Found as far south as northern Georgia, its range runs north along the Appalachian Mountains to New England and Canada's Maritimes, as well as to a few isolated populations in southern Indiana and Missouri. From its northern East Coast extremes, the ruffed grouse's range extends in a nearly continuous broad band spreading west, through the Great Lakes states and provinces out across the aspen parklands north of the prairies to the Rocky Mountains. This sweeping swath also includes the boreal forest north of the Great Lakes, reaching as far north as the southern edge of James Bay and west through the Yukon. From there, back down the ragged North American spine of the Rocky Mountains, the ruffed grouse can be found from Alaska in the north to Utah in the south. The ruffed grouse's range then hops across the mountains to the Pacific coastline, extending from extreme northern California north to Alaska. All told, the ruffed grouse has found a home in at least 38 states and all Canadian provinces and territories. Twelve subspecies of the ruffed grouse exist across this broad range, differing slightly in size, color, and food habits. These are minor differences, however, most of which are lost on all but the most fastidious of scientists.

Aspen trees, and forest disturbance, are characteristics of ruffed grouse habitat.

HABITAT REQUIREMENTS

Wherever ruffed grouse are found, it is a pretty safe bet they'll be within a short flight of an aspen tree. Considered an indicator species of the aspen-birch-fir forest type, ruffed grouse thrive best where aspen is abundant. These aspen-type forests are dependent upon disturbances that provide the opportunity for the birds to flourish. In a natural cycle, the most common cause of this disturbance is fire. Because ruffed grouse require the younger forests that sprout following a fire, they are considered a "fire-dependent" species. That's not to say they can't exist where aspen are rare, but in areas where the winters are long and harsh, stands of aspen are practically a requirement. Why?

The largest part of the ruffed grouse range lies in regions where snow covers the ground from about November until March or April. With the coming of the cold, the lush forbs of the forest floor that sustain grouse in the summer die off, and with the falling of snow, other food sources, such as acorns, are buried beneath inches or feet of the white stuff. In order to survive, ruffed grouse evolved to fit a forest type that provided a suitable winter food source. Since it is not a needle eater like its cousin the spruce grouse, it found its niche and food source in the younger deciduous forest with the nutritious buds and catkins produced by aspen and, to a lesser degree, birch.

No food source provides ruffed grouse with the needed winter nutrition better than do the buds of aspen—most notably the male aspen. These buds are high in both sugar and protein, are available in large numbers, are found on branches sturdy enough to support a bird the grouse's size, and are easy to nip from the branch. In as little as 40 minutes twice daily, the ruffed grouse can crop enough buds to sustain itself on even the coldest winter day. So it should come as no surprise to anyone that, because of this dependency on aspen buds, the range of aspen and the ruffed grouse are remarkably similar.

Good ruffed grouse country also has another important element: dense, woody cover. In the North, this dense cover usually consists of alder or young aspen, the latter of which sprout up as clones from the roots of recently harvested or burned trees. In the South, the tree species differ. There, the ruffed grouse frequently uses young stands of oak, hickory, or hawthorn. The important aspect is not so much the tree species (at least in warmer climes), but that there is sufficient dense cover comprised of sapling-sized trees or brush to protect grouse from avian predators during important parts of their life cycle.

Many mature, open forests, especially in the South where winters are mild and food is abundant year-round, could easily provide a home for grouse, yet they rarely do. Whether a ruffed grouse is drumming, feeding, sitting on a nest of eggs, or trying to raise a brood, life is tenuous. Dense cover and the grouse's own remarkable camouflage are two critical elements in its survival against predators. Open forests simply don't offer enough protection for ruffed grouse. Dense woody cover does, and dense woody cover is usually a component of young forests.

That doesn't mean that ruffed grouse are absent in older forests. Quite often, old stands are adjacent to areas that have been logged or burned within a decade or two, and some ruffed grouse will wander into

Aspen catkins are an important ruffed grouse food in the spring, as are the buds in the winter.

the older trees. And old is a relative term. Ruffed grouse clearly are dependent upon young stands of trees, but they also use forests that are "middle-aged" for certain aspects of their life cycle.

Juvenile grouse, dispersing during their first autumn, often wander long distances, passing into even very mature forests that would be unsuitable for year-round grouse residency. Thus, flushing a grouse in the autumn doesn't always indicate the presence of good habitat—with their wide wanderings, dispersing ruffed grouse can end up in some pretty unusual forest cover. But the total absence of young, dense, woody cover usually means the absence of ruffed grouse, and you won't run into a ruffed grouse in an old forest unless some younger stands are relatively near.

PHYSICAL ATTRIBUTES

In many of the places the ruffed grouse is found, it is the largest ground-dwelling bird. Although their size can vary depending upon age and sex (males are frequently slightly larger than females), most mature ruffed grouse will weigh somewhere between 17 and 23 ounces. That makes them smaller than the blue and sharp-tailed grouse, but larger than the spruce grouse and white-tailed ptarmigan. Ruffed grouse have been known to live to 8 years of age, but the majority rarely make past 3. They are considered adults when they come of breeding age—one year after they are hatched.

Ruffed grouse are monomorphic, which simply means that both sexes and all ages (once adult) look alike. There are some fairly reliable means to tell the sexes and ages apart once the bird is in hand (which will be discussed later), but from a distance it is nearly impossible to tell them apart based solely on appearance. If the bird is not in hand, then only by observing behavior can we distinguish the sex. For instance, a grouse on a nest of eggs would have to be a female because males share none of these duties, and a grouse on a log drumming for a mate is a male, for females do not drum.

Aspen buds are such an important winter ruffed grouse food that the range of the bird and the tree is nearly identical.

Overleaf: Cryptic coloration allows ruffed grouse to escape detection.

The camouflaging effect of the ruffed grouse's plumage is a marvelous example of what scientists term "cryptic coloration." Three factors make the ruffed grouse virtually invisible to the human—and predator—eye. Its protective coloration, with its subtle tones of brown, tan, black, and gray, are the very colors of the forest floor. Like many other animals, the underside of the ruffed grouse is lighter than its back, which helps disrupt the effect of its own shadow, and is called countershading. Finally, the bird's silhouette is broken by the pattern of its feathers and the light and dark areas within each. Called disruptive coloration, this combination of light and dark spots and streaks, is the effect that humans try to mimic when they manufacture camouflage clothing. Together, if the grouse remains motionless, these three factors allow it to hide in plain sight on the forest floor.

In addition to covering its body and wings, the feathers of a ruffed grouse extend down from its forehead over its bill, which is brown, thick, and curved. These feathers actually cover the bird's nostrils, and help to

Pectinations—the rows of tiny winter-growths on the edges of a ruffed grouse's toes—may help them walk on snow or grip icy branches.

warm the winter air before it is inhaled. They also make the bill look shorter than it really is. The bill is specifically designed for feeding on buds, seeds, and fruits. Although ruffed grouse have no teeth, the wide range of movements facilitated by the muscles controlling the beak allow it to grasp, nip off, and otherwise separate, divide, and swallow foods.

Unlike the legs of pheasants and other related birds, those of a ruffed grouse are covered with fine, wispy, gray feathers, all the way down to the ankle, or tarsi. This, too, is an adaptation for cold weather, and is common to all grouse. Ruffed grouse spend much more time using their legs than they do their wings, and although they don't have the great speed of a running pheasant, they can run very fast when need be. When dispersing or traveling to a feeding area, grouse frequently walk rather than fly.

The ruffed grouse's gray-blue feet are bare. They have three forward-pointing toes and one rear-pointing toe, each tipped with a short, slightly curved nail. Come winter, the ruffed grouse's toes grow numerous rows of nubs along the outside edge called pectinations. Long thought to be a winter adaptation to allow grouse to walk on snow—snowshoes, if you will—these growths, speculated famed ruffed grouse researcher Gordon Gullion, were more likely to be important aids in clinging to icy branches while feeding. In either case, these horny growths begin to grow in the autumn and are shed in the spring.

SENSES

As with most birds, the ruffed grouse's sense of sight is its most important—and it doesn't take much imagination to determine why. Picture yourself hurtling through the maze of trees and branches at 25 miles per hour and you'll have some clue as to why keen eyesight, combined with swift reflexes, is important.

Eyesight is also important to finding food, and then securing it. Grabbing food with one's mouth, without the use of hands, requires good depth of field and binocular vision. The ruffed grouse possesses both, as well as keen color vision, and it is sight that provides the grouse with most of the information of its world. Sight also controls the mating cycle of the grouse, since males perform physical displays, rather than

auditory ones, like the bugling of a bull elk. So important is this sense that most of its skull is given over to orbs for its eyes and filled with a midbrain region that "digests" what its eyes see.

The ruffed grouse's optic lobe is many times larger than the corresponding receptor for odors (the olfactory bulb), which indicates that the sense of smell is less important by comparison. And although the ruffed grouse certainly can hear, the structure of its cochlea, which processes sounds, is only about one-tenth the size of that found in a similar size mammal, leading scientists to believe that its hearing is less acute.

Of course, grouse must hear *something,* or the drumming of the male, which calls mates and repels rivals, would be pointless. It is more likely that grouse hear differently than mammals, since even though their cochlea is smaller, it possesses more hairy receptors. And grouse can hear each other's voice, as when the hen calls her chicks. But nature did not make the ruffed grouse a song bird, and it possesses neither the warbling ability of some of the other woodland birds or the capacity to gobble like the distantly related turkey. Instead, its primitive voice box is limited to making a hissing sound when the grouse is alarmed, various peeps while it is a chick, the hum of a brooding hen, a chirp not unlike the chatter of a red squirrel, and a soft, liquidy "whoota, whoota, whoota" immediately before flushing.

Finally, like most birds, ruffed grouse probably have a poor sense of taste. Rather than selecting food as we do, by how good it tastes, grouse probably select foods by sight-related clues.

RELATED TO MOOSE

Well, they really aren't related to moose, but ruffed grouse do share some interesting characteristics with the moose, deer, and elk that often share the same ecosystem, and even eat some of the same foods. All have a multi-chambered stomach and microorganisms efficient at breaking down cellulose and extracting nutrients from plants. Also, they all eat rather quickly at one spot, but move to another, safer, place to digest their foods.

The digestive system of the ruffed grouse has evolved to break down a high-cellulose diet.

Whereas members of the deer family regurgitate a bolus of food when at rest to chew it at their leisure—known to us as cud chewing—ruffed grouse, instead, store this undigested food in a widening of their esophagus known as a crop. Though different in form, deer and grouse evolved these adaptations for the same reason: storing food in a "first" chamber to be digested later allows the animal to gather and eat large quantities of food quickly without having to stand there and chew it, thus reducing the time it must spend feeding. This is a survival advantage because browsing requires that an animal or bird pay close attention to the food, reducing the amount of time looking out for predators. The "eat now, digest later" strategy increases survival odds, because the grouse can return to the safety of its roost to digest the food, similar to how a moose or deer moves off to the safety of its bed to do the same.

Eventually, of course, the grouse's food is passed down into the first of its two stomachs. This glandular stomach begins the digestive process, then moves the food on to the second stomach, known as the gizzard. The gizzard is a hard, horny gland that acts like a grindstone to break down tough cellulose fibers. Grouse, and other chicken-like birds, pick up gravel and grit that end up in the gizzard to aid in this grinding process. Finally, like the moose and deer, the ruffed grouse has a symbiotic relationship with the millions of microorganisms located in its intestines. They help the grouse extract the nutrients from its food, and these nutrients are then absorbed through the porous intestinal wall.

Since deer, moose, and ruffed grouse share similar habitats (they are often found in the same woods), and all are prey species, it probably should come as no surprise that they evolved similar processes to minimize exposure to predators while feeding and digesting. Also, their digestive tracts utilize comparable strategies and mechanisms for squeezing nutrition from similar, high-cellulose-content foods.

No, grouse really aren't related to the moose, but we can marvel at how nature has given each such similar traits.

FEATHERS AND FLIGHT

The most obvious characteristics of birds are their feathers and the ability to fly. Although ruffed grouse are swift and acrobatic fliers, they are built for short bursts of flight, not long distances.

Anyone who has dined on the delicious flesh of a ruffed grouse knows that its meat (muscle) is coarse-grained and white in color. What they may not know is that these traits belie the fact that it is a bird that spends most of its time walking, and little time flying. White muscles contract quickly, which translates into bursts of speed, and are found on birds that primarily dwell on the ground. Red muscles, like those found on ducks and geese, are fine-grained and tell of birds that fly great distances. Red muscles have more respiratory structures and contain more oxygen-carrying compounds, providing the energy needed to sustain long-distance flights. These characteristics are nearly absent in the muscles of ruffed grouse, whose flights consist primarily of short distances to feed or to evade predators.

The ruffed grouse flies only short distances, but is a master at high speed maneuvering through thick forest.

41

Of course, the ruffed grouse would have a hard time flying if it didn't have feathers. In addition to their role in flight and their camouflaging effect discussed earlier, feathers serve to protect the bird from insects and parasites, as well as from weather. They also serve as a means of sexual display.

The most conspicuous feathers on the ruffed grouse are those of the tail. When folded, the tail is long and square (about the length of a dollar bill), but when the bird becomes alarmed or is strutting for a mate, the tail can be fanned out. Unlike that of related grouse, the ruffed grouse tail has a dark broad band near the tip (called the subterminal band), which is particularly striking when the tail is fanned. In relation to body size, the tail of females is usually shorter than that of males. The pattern of markings on the tail—alternate irregular dark and light bands—is unique to each bird, as are human fingerprints.

In addition, the ruffed grouse possesses the "ruff" around its neck that gives it its name. When compacted, these blunt feathers form a

This strutting male displays his barred tail and broad "ruff,"
for which the bird is named.

roughly triangular patch at the base of the head on each side of the neck. From a distance, these feathers appear black, but close inspection reveals highlights of deep blue or violet. A minority of grouse will sport a chocolate-colored ruff. Whether the ruff is black or chocolate, it always matches the color of the subterminal band on the tail. The ruff is particularly important to the male during mating displays, when it is fluffed up and spread in an impressive "lion mane" collar. As you might suspect, because of this important role in attracting mates, males generally have larger ruffs than do females.

Like other birds, ruffed grouse shed old, and grow new, feathers in a process known as molting. The exact schedule depends a great deal upon the age of the bird, and even upon its sex.

Chicks are born with a coat of down, designed primarily to keep the infant warm thanks to the many air spaces created by its fluffy depth. The first molt begins during the chick's first week of life, to reveal its first "real" feathers—primary and secondary wing feathers that are critical to flight. Eventually, the downy coat is replaced by feathers across the entire body, giving the bird its juvenile plumage. At this point it looks very much like a smaller version of an adult. Because the bird is growing so rapidly at this stage, it outgrows these feathers quickly, and undergoes a second molt, which lasts into autumn. By mid-October, the subadult plumage is achieved, and the bird, to casual observance, is indistinguishable from an adult.

Adult grouse also molt, beginning with the coming of warm weather in spring. Females begin their molt earlier than males, shedding abdominal feathers first, which is thought to increase the transfer rate of heat from her body to her nest of eggs and is called an incubation patch. Females also incur more abuse to their feathers, since they rear their broods in thick cover, which tears and wears their coat. Males seem to replace their feathers faster than females. In both cases, the molt occurs in stages, since it wouldn't be wise to lose so many feathers at once that the bird couldn't fly or would be exposed to the elements. The molt proceeds through the summer, peaking in July and August, during which time the ruffed grouse is very shy, hiding in thick cover. By October, the molt is generally complete, although a few feathers may emerge after that.

When your ability to escape predators through flight and to ward off cold weather or biting insects depends upon a coat of feathers, it pays to take care of them. Ruffed grouse both preen and dust bathe to keep their feathers in top condition.

A gland on the rump, known as the preen gland, produces a waxy substance that helps waterproof feathers and keep them flexible. Ruffed grouse reach back and rub their beaks on that gland, and then distribute the wax on their body and wing feathers by stroking them toward the tip. The bird grasps a feather near the base and draws it through the partly closed beak, nibbling as it goes. This distributes the wax, and cleans parasites from the feathers. In order to preen its head, it must rub it on other parts of the body. Preening is done in a fairly open setting where the grouse can watch for ground-dwelling predators, but they usually are careful to select a preening site that has some overhead protection from hawks and owls.

Ruffed grouse also perform dust baths. Birds that do this usually don't bathe in water. In order to dust bathe, ruffed grouse first must loosen the soil by scratching it with their clawed toes. Usually they choose sites with loose soil, that are in the sun so that the soil is dry. Anthills, paths, or the exposed soil near an uprooted tree are favorite sites. Ruffed grouse work the loose soil into their feathers by first tossing the soil up on their backs with wings or feet, then shimmying and ruffling their feathers to let it spread and work into their plumage. Dust baths seem to help eliminate parasites, realign feathers, and keep them dry and fluffy.

MALE OR FEMALE?

Feathers can also give us a clue to the sex of a particular ruffed grouse. Tail feathers that are longer than the length of the back generally indicate a male (or cock) grouse, while the tail of a female (or hen) is usually the same length as its back. Male ruffed grouse commonly appear to be larger than females, and frequently, the barring on the female's flank feathers tends to be darker and have more contrast than that of the male's. As noted earlier, the ruffs on males are often more conspicuous.

Thanks to the sampling of thousands of tail feathers, Gullion reported that among Minnesota's ruffed grouse, if the central tail feather is less than 5-5/8 inches, the bird is a hen, but if it is longer than about 5-5/16 inches, the bird is a cock. Between those lengths, the bird may be of either sex.

These lengths are not universal, however. In Washington state, there is less distinction between male and female tail length. In southeastern Ohio, the tails of cocks may be as long as 7-7/8 inches, while females possess tails as long as 6-1/2 inches. Michigan's grouse are more similar to Minnesota's, with tail lengths of 5-1/4 inches for females, and 5-3/8 inches for males.

With so much variation, the use of tail feathers for sexual identification, while accurate within a given range or state, can be considered only a "rule of thumb" when comparing grouse from across the country. Additionally, a bird may have shorter tail feathers because they were "plucked" in a near escape from a predator. A dollar bill is sometimes

Ruffed grouse preen—using a waxy substance from their preen gland—
to keep their feathers in good condition.

used to measure plucked tail feathers. If either of the two middle plucked tail feathers is shorter than the dollar bill, the bird probably is a female. Longer, it is most likely a male. As a generality, across most of its range, a ruffed grouse with a tail feather of 5-7/8 inches or longer is probably a male; under 5-1/2 inches, it is probably a female.

These same two central tail feathers (called rectrices) have been used to diagnose sex based on their pattern. The dark, broad band near the end of these two feathers is almost always less distinct and fuzzier in pattern than those to either side. If this band is nearly as sharp as those surrounding it, the grouse is male, and if it is blurred or blotched, it is a female. This key shouldn't be taken as gospel, however. Males sometimes have blurry bands—as many as one in four. Females, however, rarely have complete bands. Thus a bird with a solid band is almost certainly not a female, but a bird with a blurry band stands a small chance of being a male.

There is one other clue feathers can provide for determining a ruffed grouse's sex. Feathers found on the ruffed grouse's lower back contain a marvelous camouflage pattern, enhanced by little white spots. Generally speaking, if rump feathers plucked from the back just above the tail have only one white spot or none, the bird is female. If there are two or more white spots, it is probably a male. Use this technique with caution, however. Although a 1975 study by Yvon Roussel and Reginald Ouellet for Fish and Game Quebec found this characteristic almost universal among the grouse they sampled, Gullion in Minnesota found the technique unreliable, noting it failed to properly identify the sex of one-sixth of the females, and about half of the males. However, combining all techniques—tail feather length in relationship to back length, measurements of tail feathers, examining the tail band for blotched or blurring on the two middle feathers, and the number of white spots on the rump feathers—should result in an accurate assessment of the bird's sex most of the time.

Although two central tail feathers—called retrices—
of males are frequently as darkly barred as the other tail
feathers, those of this male are fuzzy like those of a female.

A sure way to know is by examination of the sex organs. Located on either side of the spine, at the head end of the pair of 2-inch-long, flesh-colored kidneys, the testes of the male are small, dark gray balls. The female's single ovary is at the head end of the left kidney and appears as a clump of tiny tan grapes.

YOUNG OR OLD?

Come autumn, the year's new ruffed grouse have attained nearly the size and appearance of adults, making it difficult to tell them apart. But there is a way to distinguish between adults and juveniles that, though not perfect, works much of the time.

Both young and old grouse molt their wings' outermost flight feathers—called primaries—during the summer. Of these 10 feathers (per wing), the 2 at the leading (forward) edge are not shed by juvenile birds. This means that they will appear to be more worn than those new feathers found on adults. If the trailing edge is smooth and the tip curved, it

By eight weeks, young grouse sprout subadult plumage,
which resembles that of the adult.

indicates new growth, and thus an adult. If the tips are pointed and the trailing edges are ragged and worn, then they are old feathers on a juvenile grouse.

If you're still unsure, the quill will give a clue. Since feathers erupt from a sheath, new feathers (i.e., those on adults) have a flaky residual amount of sheathing remaining on them. Quills of a juvenile grouse, which does not molt these two leading-edge primaries, do not have this sheathing.

COLOR PHASES

Most people quickly notice that although all ruffed grouse are well camouflaged, not all ruffed grouse look alike in color. Some are predominately gray, some predominately brown (sometimes called red), and some are intermediate between these colors. The variety of coloration is known as color phase, and it is most noticeable in the tail feathers.

Depending upon where they live and the type of habitat in which they are found, ruffed grouse exist in several color phases, from gray to red.

Color phases and their infinite combinations can exist in any one local population, but there is usually one phase that is predominant within a region. For instance, the brown phase is dominant on both the Atlantic and Pacific coasts, while the gray phase prevails in Alaska and the Yukon. In the Southeast, brown birds are again the most common.

Scientists think color phase may be related to climate—gray phase birds may be better adapted to cold temperatures because it is suspected they have lower energy demands. Dark brown phase birds seem to do better in moist areas, while light-colored phases prevail in dry regions.

Predation rates also seem to play a role. In the North, autumn and winter ground cover of fallen birch and aspen leaves is primarily gray, giving the gray phase bird an advantage over a red phase grouse (remember, hawks and owls have very good color vision). Red or brownish grouse blend in better farther south, where leaf litter has a predominately red or brown hue.

Whether the reasons are camouflage or energy demands, Gullion's studies in Minnesota found that after the severest winters when ruffed grouse numbers drop, gray phase grouse predominate. And when the ruffed grouse population rebounds, the percentage of brown phase birds increases. Thus, in years when the majority of ruffed grouse are gray, it represents a low in the cycle, and when the red-brown birds flourish, the cycle is nearing its high point. This trend may apply to other ruffed grouse populations in similar climatic conditions across the Great Lakes region.

Considering the broad geographic range of the ruffed grouse and the variety of climates in which it thrives, it probably should come as no surprise that nature would have provided them with a nearly infinite variety of color phases through which they might better hide, more quickly dry their feathers in moist climates, repel the noonday heat, and absorb the pale warmth of the winter sun. And it should also not surprise us that they are rarely easy to classify as truly gray or truly brown. "Split-phase" birds abound. Indeed, the legendary Gullion found 30 different color variations in Minnesota alone, and across the Midwest, some 58 variations in tail color are noted!

Gray phase grouse may be better adapted to
cold weather than red or brown phase ruffed grouse.

CHAPTER THREE

In Its Forest Home
Range, Diet, and Predation

IT WOULD BE EASY for us to imagine that the ruffed grouse—or most other birds and animals—simply wander around in the woods, taking what comes their way in the matters of food, shelter, and mates. After all, the forest is no longer our home, and to many of us a tree is a tree is a tree. We tend to appreciate forests for either the beauty or commodities they supply. We tend not to think of how complex the relationship between forest and animal can be. A ruffed grouse seemingly ought to be able to survive in just about any forested cover. But nothing could be further from the truth.

To humans the forest may look relatively uniform, but for the ruffed grouse, various portions of it provide for specific needs—there are "grocery stores" and "residential areas," "day-care centers," and even "singles bars" where they look for mates. Some areas are used year-round, others serve a particular purpose for short periods of time, and the places grouse visit will vary by sex—males and females have different needs. Most ruffed grouse will spend their entire adult life in an area of less than 40 acres. Within this limited area they must meet all their needs or perish.

Good ruffed grouse habitat contains many required features—drumming logs, nesting areas, and reliable food sources.

The area that encompasses the total movements of a grouse in a year is typically called its "home range." Home ranges provide all the resources a grouse requires, but are not normally defended against other ruffed grouse. Indeed, the home ranges of several birds—especially hens and immature males—may overlap, particularly when good food sources are on the edge of different home ranges. A hen's home range may overlap the territories of two or three males.

"Territories" are different from home ranges and are limited to males. They are smaller areas—6 to 10 acres in size—that ruffed grouse males defend against intrusion by rivals. This defense consists largely of drumming, strutting, and displaying, but sometimes results in "cock fights." These movements are most obvious within a male's "activity center," which has as its focal point his drumming log. A male grouse may have several drumming logs, which are those places where he puts on his mating display each spring to attract mates. Drumming, however, isn't limited to springtime, and male ruffed grouse will defend this territory against rivals any time of year. The reason is simple: the single most important aspect of a male ruffed grouse's life is to live long enough to pass on his genes to as many mates and for as many years, as possible. Good activity centers not only have a good drumming site that contains the characteristics necessary to effective mating displays, but also must provide good protective cover and ready access to nutritious foods. As you can imagine, this center plays an important role in the male's survival and, thus, the chance to pass on his genes. It makes sense, then, that a good site would be worth defending, for these sites are not uniformly scattered through the woods.

Although a hen ruffed grouse also strives to pass on her genes, her needs in the process are quite different. Her role is to raise as many successful broods as possible. To do so, her cycle demands both a place to nest and a place to raise her offspring. The qualities that make good nesting cover and brood-rearing areas are different from those that comprise a male's territory. Whereas the male benefits by being somewhat conspicuous—his drumming and strutting both attracts mates and thwarts rivals—females benefit by being much less visible. Tending to chicks in a forest full of predators dictates both dense hiding cover and quiet behavior.

For both sexes, all of the activities and all of the kinds of habitat they need must be in close proximity to each other or the birds will fail. In addition, the habitat of one sex must be near the habitat of the other sex for procreative purposes.

On a brief walk in the woods in good grouse country—say just a half mile or so—you likely will walk through not just one example of each type of habitat, but several. Yet ruffed grouse don't exactly live on top of each other or in large groups. Except when mating, challenging a rival, or raising a brood, ruffed grouse are fairly solitary creatures, each needing its own place—and space—to thrive. Males in particular, because of their need for unchallenged drumming sites, require spacing. You can easily see, then, that if habitat is limited, there will be a limited number of birds.

For male ruffed grouse to be competitive for mates,
they must have a quality drumming site.

And, of course, in addition to good drumming logs or nesting sites, the birds must have easy access to nutritious foods. A ruffed grouse could probably find enough to eat just about anywhere during the summer and autumn when dozens of food items are available. When winter comes, however, it brings with it new challenges and constraints, and the ruffed grouse in much of its range is limited to just a few food sources. Ruffed grouse do not migrate. So, once they have found a suitable habitat, ruffed grouse don't wander very far in the course of a year. Thus, good summer habitat also has to be adjacent to good winter habitat.

THE ASPEN–RUFFED GROUSE RELATIONSHIP

Throughout most of the ruffed grouse's range, aspen is its single most important food source, particularly during late autumn and winter. Gullion suggests that where ruffed grouse exist outside the range of the aspen species, they are living in places that should be considered peripheral to their primary range. This doesn't mean that ruffed grouse subsist solely upon aspen buds or flowers. Indeed, they may eat as many as 100 types of plants during the course of a year. But winter survival in much of the ruffed grouse's range practically demands the availability of aspen buds, and those regions of North America where ruffed grouse exist at the highest densities always are found in an aspen-type forest.

So closely are aspen and ruffed grouse associated, that the continental range of the bird and trembling *(Populus tremuloides)* and large-toothed *(P. grandidentata)* aspens are almost identical. In addition, where aspen forests exist along with other forest complexes, ruffed grouse show a decided preference for aspen. Wisconsin researcher John Kubisiak noted four times the density of ruffed grouse in aspen stands than in nearby oak forests, in part because aspen stands provided the habitat components needed.

It is important to remember that aspen forests are an "early successional stage" forest, dependent upon disturbance, and are but one stage in the progression of tree species that will inhabit a particular site over the course of centuries. Ultimately, in some natural scenarios, many of these

This grouse's crop reveals it had been eating aspen buds as well as birch catkins.

Overleaf: The densest populations of ruffed grouse are always found in aspen forests. Aspen provides food in winter, as well as dense vertical cover for nesting and brood rearing.

sites would convert to coniferous forests (pine), typically the longest-lived species in these regions. Without disturbance, pine forests would eventually take over aspen stands if there were both nearby pine seed sources and long periods of time between disturbances. These intervals between disturbances allow young pines to first take root beneath the aspen cover and then to grow through an aging and decaying aspen stand, which falls apart as it gets old, opening the forest canopy. This opening gives the conifers the sunlight they need to grow and take over the site. Aspen forests may subsist at a site for generations if the forest is periodically disturbed. If the aspen forest is logged or burned before the pine forest establishes itself, then a new, younger aspen forest will be born.

In other words, those portions of the primordial forest that consisted of large pine were not good ruffed grouse habitat. Ruffed grouse existed in those regions, though, because fire or other natural incidents (disease or wind) periodically opened up the forest canopy to allow young aspen forests to pioneer. When Europeans arrived and began

A mixture of both young (nesting, rearing sites) and middle-aged (food source) aspen makes the best ruffed grouse habitat.

widespread logging, the amount of old growth diminished. In the aftermath, the number of acres that became better suited for ruffed grouse increased, as did ruffed grouse numbers.

In addition to being a critical food source, aspens also provide important habitat. Because aspen grow as clones—new, genetically identical same-sex trees sprout from the roots of a harvested or burned aspen—they form incredibly dense stands of saplings during the first few years. With as many as 70,000 stems per acre in the first year, the stand begins to thin out over time as weaker saplings die.

By the time the stand is 4 years old, it becomes brood-rearing habitat—dense enough to thwart predators, but open enough to provide sunlight to grow herbaceous foods on the forest floor. When this same stand reaches 8 years of age, drumming males as well as hens with broods find it attractive. By 11 or so years of age, this stand will consist of excellent vertical cover, which is so important in protecting the ground-dwelling ruffed grouse from hawks and owls. It is excellent habitat for both sexes because it is open enough to encourage an abundance of forest floor plants, which provide spring and summer foods. Until this stand is about 30 years of age, when stems per acre have dropped to about 2,000 through natural competition for sunlight, it remains good ruffed grouse cover. Stands older than this become less desirable grouse habitat, but it is important to note that these older aspens are the ones that produce the flower buds useful as winter food. If the stand is not destroyed by logging or fire, it will, within another 30 or more years, decay, allowing the next successional stage—probably pines—to replace it. At that point it will become unattractive to ruffed grouse.

There is a common misconception, probably based on misinterpretation of Gullion's landmark research, that ruffed grouse thrive only in young aspen forests. This is a limited truth—neither a uniformly young nor a uniformly old forest benefits ruffed grouse because the bird's needs change during various times of the year. Because the older trees produce the kind of buds ruffed grouse need to survive in the winter and young stands of aspen provide the kind of cover preferred by broods, good grouse cover must have both. In addition, stands of 8- to 10-inch-diameter, pole-sized aspen—neither young nor old—provide excellent cover for the drumming male ruffed grouse.

Obviously, then, in order to have large numbers of ruffed grouse, a forest must not only be "young" overall (i.e., early successional stage), but, within that stage, have a diversity of year classes. This kind of diversity often results from forest fires, which leave a "mosaic" of ages as wildfire follows the contours of hills, burning more intensely in dry areas and more slowly in (or skipping) wetter areas, or even jumps from one place to another, thanks to wind. When planned carefully, logging can also simulate this type of mosaic pattern.

WINTER FOODS

So why is the aspen so important as a winter food source? The answer lies in its flower buds—and not just any bud, but the bud of the male aspen.

The flower bud of the male aspen contains relatively high amounts of proteins, fats, and minerals. Studies have shown that even with the availability of other foods, ruffed grouse tend to favor male aspen buds disproportionately. Fortunately for ruffed grouse living in areas of prolonged snow cover (which buries foods on the forest floor), these buds are both abundant and nutritious. So important are these older trees and their buds that when these trees are cut down, drumming sites in the vicinity are soon abandoned. The buds of the female aspen, by the way, are smaller, poorer in nutrients, and consequently little used by ruffed grouse. Ruffed grouse tend to favor the buds of male trembling aspen over those produced by the large-toothed aspen.

Not only are male aspen buds nutritious and abundant, they grow on a tree ideally suited for browsing. The branches of aspen are fairly stout, allowing a bird the ruffed grouse's size to perch and feed with little fluttering and flapping—the kind of movement that attracts predators and increases heat loss. Ruffed grouse seldom feed in aspen trees less than 30 years old. This propensity may have something to do with the limb stoutness of older trees or the vigor of their buds. In addition, aspens growing under some kind of stress (disease or damage by wind or fire) produce more buds and are correspondingly favored by ruffed

Winter snows cover the foods found on the forest floor, making the nutritious buds of the male aspen a critical winter food source.

grouse. Flower buds near the crown of the tree also tend to be larger and more nutritious and, again, are favored foods. Gullion reports that a "browse line" appears on the upper one-third of many of the trees he monitored during research.

Come spring, the catkins—the long, soft and fuzzy "flower" produced by the aspen bud—become a short-lived but important food. In fact, as long as snow lingers on the ground and green-up has yet to occur, catkins may be the only food available to ruffed grouse for most of a month.

In other areas where aspen is less abundant, the buds of other trees have to do, such as those of the black cottonwood in western Washington. Ruffed grouse can also survive, but in lower densities than in areas with aspen, on the catkins and buds of black cherry, apple, hazel, birch, ironwood, and willow. At one time in parts of New England, bounties were placed on ruffed grouse because they ate the buds of valuable apple trees.

The buds and catkins of some of these trees—most notably the ironwood and birch—are on the end of long slender branches frequently barely sufficient to hold the weight of a grouse. This requires much more flying and flapping for the browsing ruffed grouse, possibly attracting predators and burning up critical winter energy, which partially explains why they don't do as well on a diet of these buds. In addition, the buds of some of these other tree species are also much smaller than those of the aspen, and so the grouse must expend considerably more time and energy in feeding, receiving less for its effort. It is easy to see why ruffed grouse naturally select the more nutritious, more abundant buds on the stout limbs of aspens. But even in areas where aspen are abundant, ruffed grouse must occasionally turn to these other winter food sources since aspen bud production isn't uniform from year to year. In years of low aspen bud availability, the other tree species help preserve the population of ruffed grouse, but they will decline in number and survivors will weigh significantly less than normal come spring.

If northern ruffed grouse in winter are primarily "florivorous" (flower eaters), their southern counterparts are mostly "herbivorous" (plant eaters). South of the range of aspen and of persistent snow ground cover, grouse continue to feed primarily on forest floor foods like evergreen leaves and ferns, which persist in winter. Some favorite foods are greenbrier, Christmas fern, and mountain laurel. While it may seem that these grouse have an easier time in winter than their northern relatives, in fact this diet is very low in proteins and fats, leading some researchers to believe that the Southeast region's grouse population is limited by these nutritionally inadequate foods. Acorns would provide a more nutritious winter supplement in the South and, indeed, they are a favored food when available. But ruffed grouse must compete with the more numerous white-tailed deer and squirrels for this food source. In addition, the best producers of acorns are older trees, which typically exist in stands that are very open and "park-like," leading to high predation rates.

Fall ripening berries, like these of the dogwood, help provide a varied menu.

OTHER FOODS

If winter is a time of relative food paucity, the coming of spring, the lushness of summer, and the bounty of early autumn give grouse a wide range of food choices. Some 100 types of plants have been noted in the ruffed grouse's diet.

While we don't normally think of birds as browsers, this is an accurate term when describing ruffed grouse. They are opportunistic feeders, and almost all feeding is done on the ground during the snow-free months of the year. In the spring, ruffed grouse switch from feeding in trees on buds and catkins, to feeding on the leaves of strawberry, bunchberry, coltsfoot, dandelion, fern, or those of a myriad other plants. By the end of spring, as much as 80 percent of a ruffed grouse's diet will be made up of green leafy vegetation. Early ripening seeds and fruits also appear in their diet.

Young ruffed grouse hatch in late spring and early summer, and these hatch dates coincide with the emergence of insects. Since a ruffed grouse chick is not physically capable of feeding on plants for the first month of its life, it will exist almost solely upon insects and small invertebrates—and it isn't choosy. Whatever will fit in its tiny beak, and whatever it can catch, ends up being eaten. Grasshoppers, ants, worms, grubs, crickets, caterpillars, and even mosquitoes are consumed with gusto. Since this is a highly vulnerable time in a grouse's life because of its small size and inability to fly, a chick's "job" is to grow quickly and attain flight feathers. This protein-rich diet is the perfect fuel for those tasks.

Because of the dense foliage of summer and the secrecy of the ruffed grouse's summer lifestyle (hens with broods tend to be very inconspicuous and molting adult birds of both sexes spend much time in protective cover), little is known about their summer eating habits. But it is safe to assume that adult ruffed grouse eat from a wide range of leafy plants, seeds, and fruits. As the chicks mature, they begin to feed less on insects and more on plants, so that by 2 months of age, bugs comprise only 30 percent of their diet.

In the lushness of summer, ruffed grouse may consume dozens of types of green, leafy vegetation.

Overleaf: For the first month of its life, a ruffed grouse chick will eat only a high-protein diet of insects and invertebrates.

Come autumn, things get even better. Acorns and other seeds are abundant and important fall foods, as are fruits. In regions where grapes occur, they are a favored selection. In the North, the berries of the mountain ash are fed upon heavily. Service berries and the fruits of cherry, hawthorn, rose, and greenbrier are regionally important staples, although the grouse also continues to eat large amounts of leafy matter through autumn.

Unlike migratory birds, which store large amounts of fat in autumn to fuel themselves through their long flight south, ruffed grouse store very little body fat. And unlike deer, which put on fat in the fall and then turn down their metabolism in winter so that they require less food, ruffed grouse must eat at least twice daily in winter to survive. Consequently, fall foods aren't important for the purpose of fat storage, but they do help the ruffed grouse to achieve its maximum yearly weight, and to otherwise put the bird in good health so that it is prepared to face winter's challenge.

Since ruffed grouse have developed a symbiotic relationship with microorganisms in their digestive tract, which allows them to process their fibrous winter diet of buds, Gullion speculated that those ruffed grouse that switched to bud eating early in the fall have higher survival rates than those that continued to feed on the "junk" foods of fruits and nuts. He wrote that those that made the switch early conditioned and developed a larger and healthier population of these microorganisms and so were better able to fully utilize winter's tough foods. He also speculated that this would lead to better winter survival rates.

CYCLES AND SURVIVAL

Living as it does near the bottom of the food chain, the ruffed grouse plays an important role as food for other animals. It is not a long-lived bird. Few will live to be 3 years old. Indeed, if 1,000 eggs were laid in spring, only about 400 of those would end up enjoying their first autumn that year. And of those, only about 180 would survive through

Although berries are a favorite fall food for ruffed grouse, Gordon Gullion considered them "junk" food, and speculated that grouse that switched to aspen buds in the fall had a higher winter survival rate.

winter to have a chance to mate for the first time come spring. Less than half of those (about 80) would make it to a second mating season. In the third spring as an adult, only 30 or 40 out of this group would still be alive, falling by slightly more than half again in the next year.

Death comes in many forms—disease, accidents, weather-related stress, and predation. Of these causes, predation ranks highest, although it is frequently difficult to separate it from the other factors. A ruffed grouse weakened by cold or disease might have died regardless of whether it had been caught by the fox or goshawk.

In addition to the annual loss of ruffed grouse, researchers, hunters, and naturalists have long noted that abundance of ruffed grouse and some other small game animals (notably the snowshoe hare) exists in cycles that last about 10 years. This cycle seems to be unrelated to the amount of food available to ruffed grouse, or differences in reproduction, leading to much speculation about its cause. The most frequently held belief is that it is related to predation. While all animal species typ-

Few ruffed grouse survive past three years of age.

ically fluctuate in number, only those whose populations rise and fall in large amounts and with regularity are considered cyclical.

There are two predation scenarios that may explain this cycle, and the "proper" one may depend upon whether or not the ruffed grouse exists north or south of the Canadian border.

Researcher Lloyd Keith's classic work *The Ten-Year Cycle* chronicled not only the periodic fluctuations of ruffed grouse, but also those of snowshoe hares, red fox, lynx, and prairie grouse. He noted some interesting findings, not the least of which is that these fluctuations are frequently related to each other and, indeed, are synchronous among species within areas. He also noted that this cycle seems to be limited primarily to the northern coniferous forests and nearby prairie aspen parklands.

Keith's research suggested the following scenario as an explanation for the ruffed grouse cycle: snowshoe hares, which are capable of breeding several times in one year, begin to increase in number. Predators that feed upon hares, particularly the lynx, goshawk, and great horned owl, find hunting easy because of the abundance of hares, and they in turn produce numerous offspring. Reproduction by the hares, however, outstrips that of the slower-to-reproduce predators, so that hare numbers continue to rise. Eventually, the hares are so numerous that they deplete their food sources, and begin to die off rapidly.

All the while hares and predators were increasing, so were the ruffed grouse because the hares acted as a prey buffer between them and the predators. But once the hare numbers plunged, the now-abundant predators must turn to other prey species—and the ruffed grouse becomes an important target. Since grouse numbers can't support a predator population as large as the one born in the aftermath of abundant snowshoe hares, ruffed grouse numbers crash, followed by a drop in the predator population. Because this cycle takes years, the woody brush that provides food for the snowshoe hare has a chance to bounce back. When it has, snowshoe hare numbers again begin to climb, and so does the ruffed grouse population, which again is buffered from predation by the numerous hares.

This classic theory holds that as long as hare populations remain high, ruffed grouse are safe. However, because the ruffed grouse is also cyclical south of the range of the snowshoe hare, some researchers began to question its validity. In the Lake States of Minnesota, Wisconsin, and Michigan, ruffed grouse follow the same or similar 10-year cycle. Yet in these regions snowshoe hares play a much less important role as a prey base. In fact, they aren't even present in some portions of these states where grouse cycles occur.

Research done in Wisconsin by Donald Rusch and others, and in Minnesota by Gordon Gullion and his team, noted that winter predation rates climbed in those years in which there were large influxes of migrating raptors (primarily goshawks). Although elevated predation rates seemed also to be the trigger for the cycle in these regions, it is a cycle unrelated to the availability of other prey in the study areas. In the Canadian example, ruffed grouse fluctuated because of the rise or fall of other prey species (the snowshoe hare) living in the same locale. In the Lake States, the fluctuation was not related to any other resident prey species, but instead to the influx of raptors. Yet, as it turns out, even these more southerly ruffed grouse cycles may be related to the snowshoe hare—but hares living far to the north. As those more northerly boreal forest hare populations decline, the hungry raptors of those regions migrate south into the northern U.S. where they feed upon ruffed grouse. Keith's model of the 10-year cycle seems valid, then, for what is occurring in Canada. And the findings of researchers in Minnesota and Wisconsin seem to indicate that the ruffed grouse cycle to the south is different from, but related to, the Canadian cycle.

Of course, nothing is quite that cut-and-dried in the world of wildlife biology. It has also been noted that ruffed grouse do not appear to be cyclical in regions outside of the aspen range. This could mean that these places are far enough removed from the Canadian cycle so that they escape its effects. But it also could indicate that the cycle may have some relationship with aspen.

When snowshoe hare populations decline, many avian predators switch to feeding upon ruffed grouse.

Gullion noted that in some winters, ruffed grouse refused to eat the buds of aspen, even though they were available to the birds. Noting that these buds have a gummy coating that contains a resin that may inhibit digestion, Gullion speculated that in years when the trees felt particularly stressed, they "protected" themselves by creating less palatable or digestible flower buds (which eventually produce the pollen by which the plants reproduce), thus ensuring their own reproduction. If this is true, then the ruffed grouse must switch to less nutritious or less abundant foods, lowering its own odds of survival. If the trees exhibit this self-defense mechanism for more than just one winter, then a cycle could be triggered. Research has yet to confirm this hypothesis.

Whatever the cause, in the region surrounding the Great Lakes, it has been noted that the cycle is generally at its low point in years that end in the number 5 or 6, and at its high point in years ending in the number 0, 1, or 2. Severe weather causing catastrophes across broad areas of the grouse range can alter this cycle. Excellent habitat can also make the cycle's peaks and valleys less distinct.

COLOR PHASE SURVIVAL

As noted earlier, most ruffed grouse subspecies come in two color phases: gray and brown (red). There are also split-phase ruffed grouse that fall between true gray and brown phases.

Gullion noted that in Minnesota, during winter influxes of goshawks or when goshawks nested in the vicinity, the brown phase grouse had a significantly shorter life span than the gray phase. Since the gray bird is always the more plentiful phase in the northern parts of the ruffed grouse range, and since these winter influxes of grouse-preying raptors is also largely a phenomenon of the northern part of the ruffed grouse range, it may suggest that the gray ruffed grouse is better camouflaged than its brown relatives. Indeed, the gray phase adaptation could well be the result of natural selection in the northern parts where the grouse are subjected to predation by goshawks and great horned owls. Conversely, when the red-brown portion of the population increases in these regions, it indicates that the cycle is on an upward trend. When only gray phase birds exist, the cycle is near its low point.

Such cycles hint at how marvelously intricate are the webs of inter-species relationships in nature. In addition to the puzzling matter of the ruffed grouse cycle, there are many nuances to what comprises good ruffed grouse habitat, not all of which are fully understood. Nature's complexity and subtlety is seldom more evident than it is in the life cycle of the ruffed grouse.

HUNTING MORTALITY

Unless predator populations become unbalanced because of some human activity, predation of ruffed grouse by raptors and mammals is unlikely to cause harm to the population. Indeed, it is part of the natural cycle.

But what about human predation upon ruffed grouse? Well, humans are predators, too, and are also a part of nature. Yet there has been concern raised over the years that modern hunting can depress grouse populations. Although the jury is out on whether this is true, it is

Hunting mortality generally has little impact on grouse populations.

safe to say that throughout most of the ruffed grouse range, hunting poses little threat to grouse numbers. And it can be equally convincingly argued that the money generated by hunting license sales actually helps to increase grouse numbers, for much of these funds are poured back into ruffed grouse habitat projects.

Hunters can, however, depress ruffed grouse numbers in easily accessible areas. Excessive road building for the purpose of timber harvest has fragmented many forests, leaving "edge" habitats that are deadly to ruffed grouse not only because of the ease of human access, but because these areas are easy places for hawks and owls to hunt. Dispersing young grouse frequently are taken unawares at such places. Overall, however, hunting mortality has low impact on grouse numbers. Recent studies in Wisconsin indicate that harvest rate by humans rarely exceeds 25 percent of the fall population of ruffed grouse. At such levels, hunter impact is minimal, since to a large degree, this harvest is what biologists call "compensatory" mortality—a great portion of the birds taken by grouse hunters would have died anyway that fall or winter.

The fact that over 30 states or provinces have ruffed grouse hunting seasons and that those populations of grouse remain stable or improve despite large harvests, indicates that hunting has little impact. Minnesota harvests some 300,000 ruffed grouse annually, and some 400,000 are taken in Wisconsin. Maine's harvest sometimes exceeds 600,000 birds. Yet in each of these states, ruffed grouse populations are healthy.

Some researchers do caution, however, that late hunting seasons (seasons that extend into winter) may cause problems. By this time of the year, the grouse that remain have found suitable winter habitat, have survived the rigors of dispersal, and stand a good chance of surviving to spring to reproduce. Late-season hunts may therefore dip into the breeding stock.

Red foxes, as well as bobcats, lynx, and other ground-dwelling predators, prey upon ruffed grouse.

CHAPTER FOUR

Spring and Summer
A Time for Birth and Renewal

FOR THOSE RUFFED GROUSE THAT SURVIVED the rigors of winter and escaped the talons of stealthy goshawks or owls, spring is a time for courtship, mating, and—thanks to the appearance of new foods—regaining lost vigor. Whereas winter serves to winnow the weak from a species' ranks, spring sets the stage for adding new recruits.

A walk in the spring ruffed grouse woods, especially in the morning, will reveal the ruffed grouse's mating drama, even if you stand with eyes closed. In the air will be heard the reverberations of the drumming of male grouse. It is a ghostly sound, for even when you believe you've located its direction or source, it seems to move again. Add to that the skittishness of the ruffed grouse, and it is a lucky person who actually sneaks near enough to see the booming ritual of this drummer in the woods.

Springtime mornings are full of the sound of drumming male ruffed grouse.

Like the bursting of buds on a warm spring day, the life of the ruffed grouse quickens in spring. The availability of other prey species, many of which had been hibernating, and the grouse's ability to better hide on a leaf-littered forest floor than against the stark white of winter, allows ruffed grouse to move around with less chance of detection. Hens travel about seeking the sources of the calls of drumming males, and cocks strut on log or rock in ritual display, revealing themselves as they do at no other time of the year. Thus, while the exposed forest floor and the bird's incredible camouflage gives the ruffed grouse an edge against predation, increased movement and the activity of the mating ritual offsets that gain, especially for males. The perennial drama of mating, birth, and death heightens the tension in the spring grouse woods, a drama that will shape the grouse population for the coming year.

DRUMMING

Moved by the need to pass on his genes, the male ruffed grouse has evolved, and acts out, a magnificent mating and territorial display called drumming.

It is no coincidence that the ruffed grouse has chosen an auditory signal to achieve this goal. Living as it does in dense forest that limits visibility, colorful displays—such as those of the drake mallard or other male ducks—would be an inefficient means of attracting a mate. Neither would an aerial display serve his needs, as it does the male woodcock that shares his woods. The ruffed grouse is neither small enough nor fast enough to accomplish this aeronautical task. Sound is the tool he uses to convince hens to visit him and see his display.

Other forest species use similar tactics. The bull elk, for instance, bugles on chill autumn days to audibly attract mates and deter his rivals. The wolf, with its howl, marks its territory with an audible "fence." So too the male ruffed grouse signals both his readiness to mate and his willingness to defend his territory by drumming. This activity helps to ensure that, in contiguous grouse country, males are equally distributed—a sensible and beneficial evolutionary trait, for it provides relatively easy access for females seeking a mate. Were males to gather in groups—as does the related sharp-tailed grouse of the prairie—females would have to travel longer distances, exposing themselves to predators. This spacing of males means that each female's territory overlaps at least one male, and perhaps as many as three, allowing her to safely find and choose a mate. Gullion notes that in good grouse country, males each dominate an area of about 10 acres, and are distributed approximately 150 yards apart.

Drumming occurs year-round, indicating that it is more than just a tool to attract mates. Although the fervor of drumming is never more pitched than in late winter and early spring, it can occur in any month of the year. The only time it comes close to rivaling its springtime intensity, however, is in the autumn, and this makes eloquent sense if one stops to consider it. In the fall, young males are dispersing from their mother's home range, each seeking to secure a territory of its own. Adult males with established territories—in which they live their entire lives once acquired—drum frequently in September and October to let the young

The large pile of grouse droppings shows that this log is a well-used and much-favored drumming site.

males know they'll harbor no rivals. As with most species, nature has provided ruffed grouse males with this clever way of defending their territories that falls short of actual combat, since such territorial battles could leave one or the other rival injured, threatening the combatants' ability to mate. Whether it is the ritual bugling of a bull elk or the drumming of a ruffed grouse, territories are therefore defended without physical contact, although combat between rivals of near equal status can occur.

As the snow melts, and particularly when drumming sites (most frequently, a log) become exposed, the cock grouse moves center stage. Indeed, the very spot on which he drums—a mere foot or so of space on the log and a place he returns to each time—is called the drumming stage. The actual time of year this event takes place differs with latitude. In the southern parts of ruffed grouse range, mating drumming can begin in late March, peaking sometime in the second week of April. Farther north, the stage is set a bit later. In Minnesota, for instance, peak drumming times occur a few days either side of April 29. The majority of drumming done during the peak periods is executed by males that had established their territories the previous fall. When their peak drumming period has ended, these males will drum only infrequently over the next 2 weeks. However, after this 2-week period has ended, a second drumming peak occurs, one performed primarily by the younger, less established males. Previously unable to compete with their older rivals, these young males have not had a chance to mate.

Since weather can vary dramatically at this time of year—in some warm years plants will already have begun to bloom, while in other years, traces of snow can still be found—drumming does not seem to be related to either plant phenology or the complete lack of snow. This suggests that photoperiod, which is the ratio of the length of daylight to dark hours in a day, is accountable for triggering hormonal responses in the male ruffed grouse, thus stimulating him to these peak drumming events. This phenomenon is common to many species. For instance, photoperiod governs the growth and shedding of antlers in deer, elk, and moose, and the mating rituals of black bears, trout, and salmon.

Male ruffed grouse are territorial, and this male surveys his domain from his drumming log, watching for rivals, mates, and predators.

Overleaf: Using his tail as a brace against the log, this red phase male drums to attract mates.

Regardless of why or when drumming occurs, the mechanics of it are always the same. The male grouse moves to his drumming stage and, with his claws, tightly grips the stage's surface. He also fans and drops his tail to the surface, using it as a brace and counterbalance, without which he might actually drive himself off the log during the drumming cycle.

We've all heard the old wives' tale that a drumming grouse beats his wings against a hollow log to produce the sound he makes. That, of course, isn't true, because at the very least, we know that not all logs are hollow, or that all drumming stages are logs. The truth is that the cock ruffed grouse quite rapidly beats his wings and, in that flurry, creates a vacuum and a miniature sonic boom. It is the air rushing in to fill the vacuum's void that creates the startling drumming sound. To a great many people, drumming sounds like a small two-cycle gasoline engine starting.

It wasn't, in fact, until the advent of high-speed photography that researchers really began to understand the mechanics of drumming. To the unaided eye, drumming occurs too rapidly to see what is really

The drumming sound is the result of miniature sonic booms,
as the bird beats his wings fifty times in ten seconds.

happening. Amazingly, photography has revealed that a ruffed grouse beats its wings somewhere between 45 and 50 strokes in the average drum, which lasts only 8 to 10 seconds. No wonder we couldn't see what was going on! It also appears that drumming, while instinctive in origin, requires experience to master. Some young males have been observed furiously going through the drumming motion without making the drumming sound.

Although drumming can occur at any time of the day, most of it takes place in the early morning hours either side of sunrise. It isn't unusual, however, for males to move to their drumming stage in the middle of the night. Dr. Herbert Archibald's work, done in central Minnesota using radio-tagged grouse, found males on their logs in the middle of the night, with a majority of their drumming occurring just before sunrise. Other researchers have noted that nighttime drumming is more frequent when there is a full moon. Weather can also affect the drumming time and interval. For instance, spring snowstorms or heavy rain will interrupt drumming, although misty days seem to have little effect. Foggy days generate high drumming activity, perhaps because of the efficient manner in which sound travels under these damp conditions. Although wind doesn't inhibit drumming, it does make it more difficult for us to hear it, and perhaps even for the female grouse to hear it as well.

Research done in North Carolina by Steven Stafford, while pursuing his master's degree at the University of Tennessee, indicates that drumming intensity is highest on mornings with temperatures that begin around 25 degrees F and are rising rapidly. Once the temperature reaches 42 degrees F, drumming activity drops off dramatically. At night, the interval between drumming flurries averages about 5 minutes. As daybreak arrives, drumming activity increases in intensity, with only a brief rest of 3 or 4 minutes between drums. As the morning progresses, the intervals between drums lengthen, perhaps signaling that the bird is tiring. Males may even occasionally stop to feed during a bout of drumming.

Some evidence indicates that there is competition between drumming males. The more males in the area, the more furious is the drumming. Some birds have even been observed responding to a neighbor's drum by mimicking the rival's intervals, or by beginning drumming as soon as they hear the rival start. These events, called "drumming duels," tend to be longer in duration and more fierce than a normal drum. This may simply be an automatic reflex, since hormones are running high, stimulating territorial behavior. Or it could be an attempt to "drown out" the rival's drum, in an effort to distract females.

Gullion also noted that particularly dominant males may actually attract other males, in addition to females, to their drumming site. These other males, most likely aggressive younger birds, drum on the periphery of the dominant male's territory, perhaps in the hopes that they will be able to displace the older male, or waylay one of the females he may attract. In the case of such drumming "clusters," males may be spaced only 30 or so yards apart, instead of the more typical 150 yards.

In case studies where the dominant male has been purposely trapped and removed, or was killed by predators, an alternate drummer will frequently quickly move into this dominant drummer's place, usurping his prime location. These birds typically drum very little prior to the removal of the dominant bird, seemingly "hanging around" hoping for just such an opportunity to inherit a quality drum site. In years when grouse densities are high, two males may even share the same activity center, drumming within sight of each other on nearby logs. Called "satellite drummers," neither male is dominant, and they exist as rivals.

Whether male grouse are drumming alone, in clusters, or as rivals, this is an activity that is arduous. In addition to the energy burned in drumming, males also spend less time feeding. The result is that by the end of the spring drumming season, a male ruffed grouse may lose 10 percent of his body weight.

Not all drumming sites are logs—this male drums on a moss-covered rock.

DRUMMING COUNTS

The secretive and camouflaged ruffed grouse would seem to be a bird for which population numbers would be difficult to discern. But thanks to the vigorous drumming of male ruffed grouse, wildlife managers have a tool to survey grouse populations.

In much of ruffed grouse country, wildlife managers conduct spring surveys known as "roadside drumming counts." These counts take place on established transects in grouse country. Wildlife managers drive these routes each year, stopping at prescribed places where they pause to listen for drumming males. Most of these counts are done during the peak time of the day—from just before sunrise until about 2 hours later—and during the peak of the drumming cycle. The total number of drums heard during a 4-minute interval are noted, giving an estimate of the number of males in that area. The researcher then moves on to the next stop, usually about a half mile away, and repeats the process.

Of course, not all males drum (young males may not have a territory), and the drumming count can't assess the number of females in the population. In addition, weather can affect how many birds are drumming on a given day, or if they can be easily heard. And counts taken later in the morning tend to reveal fewer drumming males than those taken near sunrise because activity decreases. Nonetheless, drumming counts are the best tool available for estimating ruffed grouse numbers, and biologists are well aware of the flaws. Drumming counts are not held up as actual population numbers, but instead are fairly accurate reflections of population trends. To that end, they are a useful tool, and are conducted in almost all of the Great Lakes states, Manitoba, Ontario, and parts of the East.

ACTIVITY CENTERS AND DRUMMING STAGE

The location for all this furious drumming is called the drumming stage, and it is located near the center of the male's activity center.

A male ruffed grouse's activity center can be as small as 5 acres or as large as 30, and can be considered his territory, although there is little evidence that he actively physically defends its entire area. As noted earlier, the drumming itself tends to ward off many rivals. Most physical territorial defense takes place at or near his actual display site, or drumming stage; he may have one, two, or even three stages.

Activity centers need to have more than one habitat component. In addition to one or more drumming stages, the site needs to have access to foods (most drumming logs are within, or near, a stand of male aspen trees) and to possess just the right balance between dense overhead cover and surroundings open enough so that the male's drumming and strutting can be observed by females.

The actual drumming site is obviously crucial to the activity center. Male grouse prefer a log that is about 15 inches above the ground and about 20 to 40 feet in length. The site will typically contain fairly dense vertical cover extending 10 to 20 feet above the log, which provides protection from avian predators. Drummers also need a clear escape route should they need to flush quickly. A majority of drumming logs will have a root mass, a stump, or a clump of brush on one end, which also serves as a guard object to protect the bird from predators.

Since drumming can attract predators as well as mates or rivals, during pauses between drums, males carefully observe their surroundings.

If overhead cover is needed to protect the drumming grouse from hawks and owls, then a relatively clear forest floor beneath is crucial to watch for foxes or bobcats. Gullion notes that over 70 percent of the drumming logs he examined had no objects within a 50- or 60-foot radius large enough to conceal these four-footed predators.

A male's most favored drumming site is called a "primary" log. If a grouse has a second or third drumming log, termed an "alternate" log, it likely won't meet all the just mentioned habitat requirements quite as well as does his primary log. Despite the poorer quality of these sites, drummers may use them in an attempt to lure females that live nearer those sites, or to engage nearby males in drumming duels. Gullion calls such logs "challenge" sites. Moving from log to log could also be a defense mechanism. Some long-lived raptors may indeed remember where a particular grouse normally spends his time. By moving, the male ruffed grouse may tend to confuse the hawk or owl.

Good drumming sites may be used for the entire life of a single grouse—which is normally only 3 or 4 years. Whether or not he remains at that site over the course of years depends largely upon its suitability. A young male ruffed grouse may not be adept at selecting his first drumming site and activity center, and may choose to move the next year. If he does, he may take over a better site formerly occupied by a dominant male that was lost to predation. Particularly good drumming sites have been occupied for generations by a succession of males utilizing the same log until it rots away, or the habitat grows up or is otherwise altered to make it less favorable. Sites that are used by one grouse for his lifetime, then abandoned, are called "transient" sites. If a log is used by a succession of males, researchers term it a "perennial" site.

Careful selection of a drumming site is important to the survival of the drumming male ruffed grouse. His mating display and drumming makes him quite visible—moreso than at any other time of the year. If he selects a site well, though, he will be quite safe. Perched and alert as he is for the presence of female ruffed grouse, he is also in the perfect position to spot predators, and is further protected by overhead cover and his

If it is a good drumming site, a male may use
it throughout his three or four years of life.

Overleaf: His careful selection of a good drumming site means
this male will survive longer and reproduce more often.

guard object. Perhaps it is nature's way to put the drumming grouse to such a test. Less astute males that choose poor and dangerous sites are probably weeded quickly from the gene pool, serving instead as dinner for some stealthy predator. Cock ruffed grouse that choose high-quality sites tend to survive to breed, thus passing on their superior genes.

It makes sense that a male with a choice drumming site—which increases survival and helps to ensure he passes on his genes—would be willing to defend it against rivals. Although his drumming tends to drive off most other males, occasionally near-equals or an aggressive youngster will challenge an established male. Such cockfights are very rare, and probably actually occur more often in the fall when young males are dispersing, rather than in the spring when most males are contemplating mating. As with other species, the larger male grouse has the advantage in a physical confrontation, and it is usually the established drummer that is larger because his territory, with all of its food and protective advantages, has aided him in living long enough to attain his full rank and large size.

When squaring off, the contestants will first go through a ritual display of strutting in an attempt to see if one or the other bird will "blink" first and back off. With their tails broadly fanned, and neck ruffs fluffed and erect, the rivals hiss and shake their heads while strutting back and forth. One or the other may attempt a short rush to see if he can drive off his opponent. If the rival won't capitulate, the birds assume a fighting posture, with head low and neck outstretched, wings back along the body, and the tail folded. An attacker will use its beak and feet as weapons. A few seconds of such scuffling is usually enough to convince one or the other grouse to leave the site.

Interestingly, a male will also use the same ritual strutting display when he sees a female approach his drumming log. The outcome, of course, is much different, as is the female's response to his strutting display.

Most drumming occurs in the hour just before, or just after, sunrise.

COURTSHIP

The male's response to any bird that enters his activity center in response to his drumming is always the same—strutting and display. Whether he gets angry, or "falls in love" depends upon the response he receives.

We already know how another male will respond to the dominant drummer's display—he'll strut too. But female ruffed grouse choose a different display, one that tells the resident male that, not only is she not a threat, she is receptive to mating. Approaching him with delicate, short steps, she doesn't fluff up her feathers or fan her tail, she slims her profile by flattening her feathers and wings and stretching out her body. In contrast to the male's tail, which will be upright and broadly fanned in display, the female's tail will be folded and lowered. At this time, a slash of bright red skin directly above the male's eye—the ruffed grouse's only concession to colorful display—will be visible, revealing his fiery passion.

Having observed another grouse approaching, this gray phase male spreads his ruff and tail in display.

Courtship is brief, and copulation even briefer, lasting only seconds. It is believed the hen is only receptive to breeding for a very short period of time, and that it ends with the laying of her first egg of the season. It is likely that she'll mate with only one male, unless she loses her eggs early in the cycle, at which time she'll seek another mate. Most female ruffed grouse probably breed when 1 year old. Indeed, males are just as likely to be sexually mature at that age too, but because they must compete with older males for mates, it is probable that many must wait until they are 2 years of age to reproduce for the first time.

Once mated, the hen will retreat to build her nest and lay her eggs, and will have no further contact with the male. Males, however, will continue drumming and guarding their logs straight through the nesting cycle, although with less intensity. One male may mate with a number of females in the course of a single spring, and by continuing his drumming into the nesting season, he'll continue to advertise his availability to hens that have lost their clutch and are seeking to mate again.

Just how late in the nesting cycle a hen will attempt to re-nest is unknown. It is known, however, that once incubation begins, hens start to reabsorb the remaining ova in their ovaries. If her clutch is lost late in the cycle, it may be physically impossible for her to conceive again. The earlier in the nesting cycle the clutch is lost, the more likely it is that hens will attempt a second. Second clutches always contain fewer eggs than the first, owing to the physiological demands of the cycle—the hen lacks the energy to reproduce with the same vigor. Ruffed grouse do not have two hatches—broods that are seen late in the summer containing chicks less mature than is normal for that time of year are the result of a re-nesting effort, not the result of a second hatch.

NESTING AND HATCHING

Once mated, a hen ruffed grouse moves off to choose a nesting site within her home range. She receives no assistance from her mate in incubating or rearing. Within a grouse population, unless a hen is unhealthy, it is likely that all are mated and will attempt to raise a brood.

This is by no means an easy task. Predators will seek out both the hen and her eggs, and should she be successful in evading them during the nesting period, she faces raising a relatively defenseless brood of chicks until they are old enough to fend for themselves.

To do so, a hen must choose her nesting and brooding areas with care. Most nesting sites are located in upland vegetation that has fairly dense overhead cover. Yet it must be open enough at ground level so that hens can spot intruders, much the same way a cock chooses his drumming site. To provide further security, hens frequently build nests against the base of some object, such as a tree, stump, or brush pile with an open avenue to provide escape. Occasionally, hens will choose a wet area to nest in, such as in an alder lowland. Hens tend to respect the boundaries of other hens, and so nests are relatively well spaced, some 500 feet apart.

A hen on a nest, unless she moves, is incredibly difficult to spot, thanks to her cryptic camouflage. There are numerous reports of foresters and biologists nearly stepping upon hens, since hens tend to "hold tight" in the face of danger unless they are certain they've been spotted. Gullion reports being able to touch nesting hens before they flee. This is an important survival mechanism to protect her eggs—as long as she sits still on the nest, both she and the eggs are extremely difficult to see. Eggs in an uncovered nest, however, are very visible.

Ruffed grouse nests are simple affairs consisting largely of a shallow bowl made from leaves and needles on the forest floor, which the hen lines with items within easy reach. Unlike some other birds, she does not contribute down or feathers to the nest, although some feathers will be naturally shed during her nesting duties. The nest is constructed simply by tossing items over her shoulder; these fall onto her back, then slip down around her, forming the bowl.

Hens begin laying their eggs within 3 to 5 days of mating. Unless she is in the process of actually laying an egg, she stays away from the nest. It takes about an hour to lay each egg. Eggs are laid at intervals of 25 to 30 hours, which means it takes about 17 days to lay an average clutch of 11. If this is her first nesting attempt of the year, the clutch will range from 9 to 14 eggs. If she loses this nest to predators, the second clutch will be smaller, perhaps only 8 eggs. She does not begin incubating the eggs until the last one is laid.

Laying eggs is an energy-consumptive task, and the hen feeds voraciously during this period. Each egg weighs about 4 percent of her body weight, and the entire clutch will be equal to about half of her weight. When laid, each egg weighs about 20 grams (or three-quarters of an ounce), is about 1-1/2 inches long, just over 1 inch wide, and in color and appearance looks much like a chicken egg.

Once the last egg is laid, hormonal changes in the hen alter her behavior. No longer does she feed heavily and move about. For the next 3 weeks she is found most of each day on the nest, during which time she barely moves. In the course of a normal day, the hen sits motionless for hours on end, only rarely picking at an insect, or adjusting herself on the eggs. During the cool hours of the night she continues to incubate the eggs, but either in the morning or late afternoon (or both), she moves off to feed. These forays—as few as 1 and as many as 5—are brief, rarely totaling more than 1-1/2 hours per day. Generally, a hen walks a few paces from the nest and then flies to nearby aspen trees

Once her eggs are laid, the hen will remain virtually motionless except when feeding for the entire three weeks of incubation.

where she quickly feeds on catkins or new leaves. She makes no attempt to cover or hide her eggs while she's away.

Most hens are successful in hatching their clutch; the success rate varies depending largely upon the quality of the habitat and nesting cover. In some areas, nest losses can be as high as 40 percent, as in the New York study by Dr. Gardiner Bump. In other places, however, it might not exceed 25 percent, and Gullion's long-term study reported an average loss of 32 percent. Across much of the ruffed grouse's range, foxes are the major nest predator, but many animals and birds—such as jays, crows, ravens, chipmunks, skunks, bobcats, and raccoons—will eat grouse eggs given the chance. Hens actively defend their nests or try to draw predators away by feigning injury. Although weather can cause nest failures, the hen's devotion to incubation provides ample warmth in all but the most exceptional of cases.

If all goes well, the eggs will begin hatching after 23 or 24 days of incubation. Most clutches hatch during the first two weeks of June at the more northerly ruffed grouse range such as Minnesota and much of Canada, and in mid-May to the south. Although the eggs were laid many days apart, hatching is synchronous, with the entire brood emerging within a few hours of each other. That means, however, that in a large clutch the entire hatching process may take 24 hours.

Hens make a soft rhythmic clucking sound during the last stages of incubation, and it is thought that this triggers the synchronous response of her offspring. The chicks become active within the egg and, using the temporary "egg tooth" on their beaks, begin to struggle to crack the egg. It is a laborious endeavor for such a small creature. When the chicks emerge they are wet and weigh only about 12 grams (or just under half an ounce) each, with males slightly heavier than females. Their first task is to dry themselves so that they don't succumb to the cold. Their downy coats at this time are buff and brown, providing excellent camouflage for the weak and defenseless chicks. The hen continues incubating until all or most of the eggs are hatched, at which time she again undergoes a hormonal change, triggering brooding, rather than incubating, behavior.

Ruffed grouse eggs are roughly the size of a small chicken egg, and require 23 to 24 days of incubation.

Overleaf: Thanks to its remarkable camouflage, if it remains motionless this day-old grouse can escape all but the most carefully searching predators.

Chick size can vary from year to year, with smaller-than-average chicks born in springs following stressful winters. These small grouse never escape winter's effect, and will be smaller than average for the rest of their life. This could be a problem for males, which compete with each other in part based on size. It is also possible that a small hen may produce smaller or less vigorous broods.

Chicks can survive for 3 days without food or water at this stage—a necessary mechanism that permits time for them to dry off and for all the eggs to hatch. Once the brood is complete and all the chicks are dry, they begin a new adventure and leave the nest site forever.

BROOD HABITAT AND DEVELOPMENT

Within hours of hatching, a brood is capable of moving fairly long distances if need be—Bump chronicled one brood that moved a half mile within a few hours of hatching. In any case, within a matter of a day or two, the hen leads her brood away from the nest site to a new area,

At about a half ounce each in weight, these day-old chicks are about to embark to their mother's brood rearing area, which may be as far as two miles away.

sometimes as far as 2 miles over the course of a week. The hen is leading them to quality brood habitat, which is typified by dense overhead cover under which the defenseless chicks can hide, and beneath which they can find food. Sapling aspen stands of 10 to 15 years of age provide the best cover, for the dense aspen leaf litter generates large populations of insects, while the numerous stems and overhead canopy shield the brood from hawks. In areas where aspen is less abundant, alder stands have been noted to be important brood areas. Fifteen-year-old stands of vegetation in mixed oak forests have also proven attractive to ruffed grouse. Brood ranges average 32 acres in size, and the family wanders through it together as a unit at a rate of about 400 yards per day. The brood will stay together for the next 17 or so weeks.

Hatching dates of May and June coincide with the emergence of new foods and insects. Young ruffed grouse feed exclusively on insects until about 4 weeks of age, a food which they learn to eat within a day of hatching. This high-protein diet allows the chicks to increase their size forty-fold before autumn. They may double their weight in just the first week! They are highly mobile within days of hatching and follow their mother, which keeps the brood together with soft calls, acting as a lookout for predators. Weather can be a significant mortality factor at this stage of chick development. Their downy feathers are not much use at shedding water, and if it is cool and wet for prolonged periods of time, chick mortality increases. The hen shelters her offspring as best she can with her body, which is sufficient protection during most cold nights and normal rain showers.

During this period, when predators appear, chicks depend upon their camouflage and an instinctive response to "freeze" when alerted by their mother. They remain motionless for 15 or so minutes while the danger passes, or while their mother leads it away using the classic "broken wing" ploy. If need be, she actually charges a predator, hissing until she turns its attention to her and away from the chicks. Dragging her wing and feigning injury, she flutters away from her brood. Female ruffed grouse are fearless in this defense tactic, often performing it mere inches from the predator's sharp teeth. Once convinced she has led the predator a safe distance, she'll flush and fly off, also in a direction away from the brood. Eventually, though, she makes the round trip back to the waiting chicks.

Trails and roads are particularly dangerous places for the brood. Normally, overhead cover protects them from predators such as the Cooper's hawk. But as the hen leads them through their territory, they may encounter the works of man and be forced to cross the open trail. Hawks learn quickly that these are opportune places to watch for grouse broods.

Amazingly, by the end of the first week, ruffed grouse chicks are capable of flight, however clumsy it might be. In addition to their downy coat, ruffed grouse are born with 7 of 10 primary flight feathers visible, and 9 of 15 secondary flight feathers in place. At the end of their first week of life—and certainly by 10 days of age—these feathers may exceed 2 inches in length, allowing a clumsy "bumble bee" flight of a few yards. I've only seen this once, and the flight was quite comical.

Entering the second week of life, young grouse continue to grow rapidly, pecking and consuming any little thing that moves—grasshoppers, ants, worms, and beetles. Flight feathers increase in size, and the down along their necks and backs is replaced with more durable contour feathers. Because they are gaining proficiency in flight, they are now less susceptible to predators, and able to take advantage of foods in trees. Males, which started out larger than females, are still ahead in the size race, and as they enter their third week of life, may outweigh their sisters by 15 percent or more.

While the young grouse grow rapidly, both hens and cocks are undergoing their molt, the males beginning in early June, the females somewhat later. All their feathers are gradually replaced, although the tail feathers molt almost all at the same time in August. At no time during the molt, however, is a ruffed grouse flightless, as is the case with ducks. And while this molt takes place, and while the active brood and busy hen scurry about the forest floor, ruffed grouse males secrete themselves in their territory, feeding to regain the weight and vigor lost during their very active spring.

It is now nearing July, and the forest's plants are emerging in a soft and digestible state. The 4- and 5-week-old ruffed grouse begins to experiment with fresh foliage as food, as well as nibble at berries. Insects become far less important at this stage, as the birds switch from being carnivores to herbivores. By 4 weeks of age, the tail of the chick, barely visible until now, is about 2 inches long. Contour feathers continue to replace down, and by week 5, chicks have their complete juvenile plumage and look very much like their mother. Young males may even play with courtship displays, fanning their tails and spreading their ruffs.

When they are 7 to 8 weeks old, the chicks look like adults, thanks to the development of their subadult plumage, which rapidly replaces the juvenile plumage they only just acquired. They are nearly adult in size as well, and fully capable of flight. At this age, should they lose their mother, the young grouse are fully capable of caring for themselves. The brood may now roost in trees, frequently in conifers, and especially at night. Attachment to the hen diminishes, and the young grouse become ever more independent.

By four weeks of age, chicks start to experiment with leafy foods, and their tail feathers grow to two inches in length. They are already accomplished fliers.

Independence comes at a cost. Predators, with their own hungry young to feed, take large numbers of ruffed grouse each spring and summer. By mid-August, some 60 percent of the grouse hatched that year will be lost. Not all of these losses are to predators. Occasionally a young, inexperienced grouse flies into trees or other objects, injuring or killing itself. When very small, they have been noted to fall into small forest pools and drown. Cold, wet springtime weather can also take a toll. In any case, it becomes clear why ruffed grouse start with such a large clutch of eggs—such high mortality rates require an ample number of "replacements" in order to ensure enough survive to reproduce.

At 11 weeks of age, juvenile tail feathers are molted, and the adult tail feathers immediately replace them, although it takes 2 or 3 weeks before they attain full size. During these same 3 weeks, with summer rapidly waning and the first hints of autumn in the nighttime air, the brood members begin to lose their attachment to each other. It is not a sudden separation, but gradually each bird becomes fully independent. They may still feed in loose groups, for whatever food source attracts one, may attract the others. And they may even roost in the same vicinity. But these groupings become more a matter of convenience than of necessity or biology.

Now, in their seventeenth week, the dogbane about them is crimson on the forest floor. Above them, the birch leaves are yellowing, and the mountain maple's foliage screams in scarlet. The surviving young grouse are now indistinguishable from adults in plumage and weight, except to those who might actually examine them in hand. Autumn is here. It is time for the young birds to disperse and start their new lives in ranges of their own.

At seventeen weeks, this young grouse, frozen in its stretched-out alarm pose, is virtually indistinguishable from adult grouse.

CHAPTER FIVE

Autumn and Winter
Dispersal and Survival

Autumn arrives in a flurry of colors. Warm days are followed by crisp nights. Leaves begin to tumble on the stiff winds of fall, and ferns, bracken, and undergrowth wither. The forest cover opens, increasing visibility for both human and animal predators.

Those young-of-the-year ruffed grouse that survived the summer will soon be, if they are not already, on their own. Inexperienced and even foolish, they now must fend for themselves for the first time in their lives. In that same grouse woods are numerous young predators; they too are afoot alone for the first time in their lives. Autumn is also the time of hawk migrations, and new kinds of more numerous avian predators will be searching for a grouse dinner. So too will humans, for autumn is the time of the traditional grouse hunting season. The autumn grouse woods is a dangerous woods. And should these young grouse make it through the warm days of fall, they will join the adults to face the rigors of the relentless winter.

If these seem like insurmountable hazards for the young birds, we are reminded that indeed they are not. Ruffed grouse have been facing such challenges for thousands of years, and have prospered. Human hunting pressure largely mimics the same natural selections made upon ruffed grouse by other predators. Ruffed grouse are equipped to handle these tests, and those that succeed add their genes to those other survivors within their race, strengthening it. Those that fail instead help other creatures succeed, becoming the gift of food.

Come autumn, young grouse disperse from the brood to find a home territory of their own.

DISPERSAL

Even as the young grouse disperse from their broods, they are not the only segment of the grouse population that faces strife. Adult males now increase their activity, for except during the spring mating season, at no other time of the year must they guard their territories so jealously. Why?

Because young males, now leaving their mothers, are seeking to set up a territory of their own. As early as the fifteenth or sixteenth week of their lives, but almost surely by the seventeenth, young grouse will begin dispersing. This is nature's way of seeding areas devoid of grouse with new recruits, places that may have newly become good grouse habitat thanks to fires, windstorms, or logging. It is also the means, over long periods of time, by which a species can slowly pioneer into entirely new regions, expanding its overall range. And it is a means by which young grouse disperse so that they avoid direct competition with their own parents or siblings for winter food. Finally, it is a mechanism that minimizes the possibility of spring matings between siblings or parent and offspring. It is a marvelous mechanism for the survival of the species. As young males disperse, they are not only seeking winter habitat, but a place to set up their own territory. Older males are busy rigorously defending their territory.

In parts of the ruffed grouse region—from Minnesota to New England and to the north—this dispersal can take place as early as mid-September. To the south of the Great Lakes region, young grouse may not begin dispersing until late October. But don't think of this as a mass exodus that occurs on a given date. Since each brood developed differently, and some may even be weeks younger than others because of re-nesting efforts, the dispersal is a drawn-out affair. Even members within the same brood may depart at different times and travel at different rates. Dispersal occurs in two stages: the gradual breakdown of the ties within the brood as the young birds become independent, followed by the final departure.

Research indicates that young males are usually the first to depart. They must find a suitable territory before winter, for it is generally the males that have become established before winter that are the most successful at attracting mates come spring. But they must find a space that is suitable both for winter survival and spring drumming, while avoiding (or contesting for) territories of older males, which do not take lightly to their trespass. These rather specific requirements may be a natural selector for early dispersal. Those that have gotten a "head start" may tend to be more efficient at finding and establishing a territory. They simply have more time to find it. Since males that have established a territory in fall are more successful at breeding, it stands to reason that they would pass on these traits. In fact, young males that do establish a territory before winter may actually start defending it through drumming and confrontation as early as late October, when they may be as young as 18 to 20 weeks of age.

In any case, dispersal comes in spurts. It is especially tentative for males. Young cocks may start out in one direction, encounter poor habitat or a dominant male, and return to their mother's brood range a number of times before they finally "cut the apron strings." Young hens, however, seem to select a direction and venture into the unknown with less hesitation. Of course, no one is bullying them along the way.

Young grouse disperse up to several miles.

While the young are off testing themselves, adult males are guarding their territories, and the now-chickless adult hens abandon their brood range and return to the place where they survived the previous winter, which is frequently in the vicinity of their nest site.

All of this shuffling about means a lot of activity in the autumn woods. Most dispersal is done in the daylight and on foot, with the young bird moving a few hundred or thousand feet per day, then lingering for a day or two. Perhaps they are evaluating the suitability of the habitat—it must contain food resources for the winter (usually aspen trees) and have those sex-specific traits they'll need in the spring. For males, that's a good activity center with drumming log (and without an already established male), and for females, the availability of nesting cover. In any case, males tend to travel about 250 yards per day, while hens wander some 500 yards at a time.

The lucky bird may find a suitable location in short order, but for others it will require several journeys. While it would be anthropomorphic to declare that young grouse are brave, certainly there is some kind of biologically driven abandon that pushes these untested grouse far from any place they've ever known into a place that may be rife with danger. As it turns out, young female ruffed grouse tend to disperse farther than males—up to 10 miles in distance, with an average somewhere around 3. Young males, perhaps owing to the fact that they need to "set up shop," usually only travel somewhere between 1 and 2 miles. Still, that's a very long distance when you consider that they move on the ground taking steps that measure but a few inches in length!

The trend for males to end their autumn wandering sooner than females is perhaps an evolved survival trait. In the spring, mortality rates for males are higher than for females, due largely to their visible and audible mating displays, which can attract predators. Females wandering greater distances in the autumn dispersal probably suffer higher mortality rates than males since they are exposed to more of the hazards of travel. Thus, the tendency for males to cease wandering sooner in autumn may be an evolved strategy of natural compensation to help balance the male-to-female ratio.

The fall shuffle is a time of high mortality for young grouse, who find themselves alone for the first time in their lives.

Overleaf: By winter, young grouse must find a place suitable for winter survival as well as spring mating opportunities.

And dispersing is a risky business. Young grouse find themselves in all kinds of habitat, some of which is decidedly unsuitable for grouse and may be too open to avoid detection by predators. They also come across the edges of farm fields, logging roads, or forest clearings. These edges are death traps for grouse, for they are frequented by many a sharp-eyed predator, especially of the winged kind. Wandering through an old forest with its open understory may similarly give a hawk or an owl a chance at a young grouse. Dispersing grouse also must navigate over or around many large woodland objects like logs, boulders, and stumps that serve as a handy hiding place for predators. Work done by Rusch and others indicates that as much as 1 percent of the grouse population per day is killed during the period of dispersal.

Gullion notes that during dispersal, it is common to find grouse in surroundings not considered good grouse habitat. This leads to confusion among hunters, many of whom have read books such as this that tout the qualities of "good" grouse coverts, yet they find birds in places

Although the broods have disbanded, grouse may occasionally be spotted together in the wintertime, attracted by food like these willow buds.

not expected. Gullion suspected that territorial males drive young males from their territory, leaving the more gregarious (i.e., tending to gather together, but not as a brood) young grouse in poorer habitats. Thus, an encounter with grouse in the autumn isn't always an indicator of the quality of habitat, the number of birds that could survive there through the seasons, or the number of birds that would be found mating or nesting in that vicinity the next spring.

AUTUMN FOODS

If there is a bit of bustling going on and a marked increase in danger in the autumn, at least ruffed grouse have one thing going for them at this time of year—an abundance of food. Acorns are falling, mushrooms are sprouting, and late-ripening species of berries, such as mountain ash, are abundant. White-tailed deer may be an ally of ruffed grouse at this time, since they can crush the stone-like acorns, and the shards they leave behind are relished by grouse. Ruffed grouse also enjoy mushrooms, but they must compete with red squirrels for this delicacy. Late-ripening berries are a choice food, and some don't even require a flight into the trees but can be picked from low growing plants, such as false lily-of-the-valley, bearberry, and bunchberry. The fruit-laden branches of the mountain ash can attract numerous grouse, and the frost-resistant leaves of clover and strawberries are also fall favorites. All in all, the abundance of fall foods makes for a diverse menu and easy pickings.

By October, however, many ruffed grouse are beginning to return to the trees to feed upon the buds of aspen or the catkins of hazel, alder, or birch. In one 40-minute period in early November, while I sat motionless in my deer stand, I watched a group of four grouse cover some one hundred yards, stopping to feed on at least five different kinds of ground-dwelling plants or their buds before they launched themselves first into some alders and, finally, into nearby aspens, feeding in both.

Because the foods of winter—buds and catkins—are more difficult to digest, requiring the aid of microorganisms within the digestive system, Gullion speculated that those grouse that switched to these foods in autumn, rather than winter, had higher survival rates. His reasoning was that since it takes time for the microorganisms to build up in the

digestive tract, those grouse that had developed healthy numbers of them were best able to wring the nutrients and energy needed from these foods. He also considered mountain ash berries and other fall fruits to be the ruffed grouse equivalent of junk food—high in sugar but low in protein.

But whether they start feeding upon aspen buds in October or November, the time will shortly come throughout much of the ruffed grouse's range that all will be forced to make the switch. Snow comes early in many of these regions and by the first weeks of November most other foods will lie beneath the first snows of the year. The young survivors of the fall shuffle, and the adult birds as well, will have settled into winter habitat. Those that wisely chose their winter cover stand a good chance of faring well. Those that did not may not see spring.

WINTER

In the whiteness and the silence of the northern winter, the ruffed grouse goes about its business, which is largely finding something to eat while avoiding being the food for others. If you follow the single-file, three-toed tracks of ruffed grouse in the snow you will see that, at least on the warmer winter days, they do not sit still, but wander within the few acres of their chosen winter home, picking at low buds and flying up to high ones. For males, the winter is spent within or on the edges of their territory, which they continue to defend. Females tend to wander a bit more, but still remain within a 20- to 30-acre area.

Ruffed grouse are well adapted to winter conditions. In fact, given the right weather conditions, winter can be a time of relative ease. The feathers on their legs grow thicker and farther toward their ankles to provide better insulation. On their beaks is a similar growth of feathers expanding downward to cover their nostrils, slowing the frigid air a moment to give it a chance to warm before it is inhaled. Tiny comb-like growths on the sides of their toes, called pectinations, began growing in autumn and are by now complete, helping to increase the surface area of the feet, which may allow the grouse to stay atop the snow as if they were on snowshoes. These nubs may be more significant as a means of providing a better grip on icy branches.

After spending the night beneath the snow (note the droppings), this ruffed grouse left wing imprints as it burst into the air. The hole at the bottom of the photo is likely the entry point from the evening before.

Survival in winter requires that grouse secure three things: an adequate food source, protection from the elements, and refuge from predators. There is one strategy they employ that takes care of the last two needs: snow roosting.

SNOW ROOSTING

Perhaps the most important winter adaptation of the ruffed grouse is its habit of roosting in snow. Wherever snow cover is deep enough—and the ruffed grouse prefers roosting snow of at least 10 inches in depth—nights are spent beneath the surface. Two critical things are occurring here. First, a grouse beneath the snow is virtually impossible for an avian predator to spot. And although foxes and bobcats can certainly smell them, the fact that grouse dive into the snow from above, often from the last tree in which they were feeding, means they leave virtually no trail to track and little scent to escape. Second, snow roosting helps to minimize the amount of energy a ruffed grouse must spend because it is significantly warmer beneath the snow than above. The less energy expended the less feeding a grouse must do to maintain its needs, reducing the time spent on a branch out in the open where it would be easy prey for hawks.

If the snow is of the right kind (fluffy powder snow is the best), snow roosting can translate into a pretty easy winter for ruffed grouse. Hidden and warm, they enjoy a level of protection they rarely have at other times of the year. This, however, is the ideal. Rarely is there a winter when snow roosting is practical the entire season. Warm spells or the odd winter rainstorm can cause the snow to crust, making roosting impossible. Occasionally, there are winters when snow depths are insufficient, yet the temperature is extremely cold. Such combinations can prove disastrous to grouse because it requires them to roost in less secure locations and to feed more extensively. It is doubtful that a healthy ruffed grouse ever starves to death, but the exposure to cold and the subsequent extended feeding leaves them far more susceptible to predation.

Ruffed grouse enter their snow roosts by diving into the snow. Obviously, hard-crusted snow, or obstructions beneath the surface, can injure the birds. Most of the time, however, they dive into the snow and then begin to migrate beneath the surface for a distance of 3 to 10 feet. At some point, the grouse hollows out a small cavity, where it spends the night. The snow may collapse at the entrance, but apparently this causes no harm since snow of the proper density for roosting seemingly is permeable enough to allow sufficient oxygen to enter. The closed entry hole may also restrict both heat loss and the bird's scent, which might otherwise signal its presence to predators. If the collapse is along the entire route of the bird's tunnel, however, it effectively pinpoints the bird's location for predators.

Snow roosting behavior is instinctive, and the young of the year seem as adept at snow roosting as adults. It is important that they are since studies indicate that the temperature within a snow roost is significantly higher than that of the surrounding outside air. Temperatures within may warm to the freezing point, and they rarely fall beneath 20 degrees F no matter how cold the night. This represents an energy savings of 30 percent or more compared to spending the night in the open.

Ideal snow for roosting is fluffy and at least ten inches deep.

Ruffed grouse may occasionally poke their head periscope-like from beneath the snow if they are alarmed, and depart the snow by wiggling to the surface and bursting, or walking a short distance before launching, into flight. When launching themselves into the air directly from their burrow, they often leave beautiful impressions of their wings and feathers in the snow.

That temperature is an important threshold. Below it, ruffed grouse must significantly increase their energy expenditures, which requires additional feeding and exposure to predators. Being able to maintain a temperature above that threshold, then, is more than just a matter of comfort. Prolonged cold with poor roosting snow can lead to increased ruffed grouse mortality.

And what if the snow isn't deep enough, or is of the wrong consistency, or if the grouse lives someplace where temperatures drop below freezing but snow is rare? In these cases, ruffed grouse make do with roosting in dense conifers. In the North, they may roost in balsam fir or spruce, while in the mid-latitudes, cedar suffices. Tree roosting has both its advantages and disadvantages. It is never as thermally effective as snow roosting—at most, the energy savings is 20 percent. And conifers frequently house avian predators. Fortunately, the structure of conifer branches offers some protection from raptors. Grouse that spend the night in trees never completely doze off, but remain semi-alert. Occasionally they make a nest on the snow's surface, hunkering down below its edge. This may actually be more thermally efficient than tree roosting because they are less exposed to air currents, but it is likely the least efficient type of roost when it comes to thwarting predators.

WINTER FOODS

The menu of autumn is gourmet but the entrees in winter are very limited in variety. Simply put, the vast majority of ruffed grouse subsist solely on buds during the winter, and mostly aspen buds at that. There are, of course, exceptions to that rule, as noted earlier. Ruffed grouse in the Southeast and other warmer climes have the choice of dining upon

Without deep roosting snow, grouse must spend the night on the ground or in a conifer tree—both of which require increased energy expenditures and also pose higher risks of predation.

Overleaf: Twice a day, grouse will fly to nearby trees to feed on buds.

the evergreen leaves of some ground-growing plants. But where snow and cold are factors, the buds of aspen or its closest relatives are the staples that fuel winter ruffed grouse survival.

Male bigtooth and quaking aspen beyond 30 years of age produce the best-quality flower buds and are favored by ruffed grouse whenever they are available. The catkins and buds of younger aspen, birch, hazel, ironwood, or willow are supplemental to this diet, and grouse densities are lower in regions where these are the only foods available. Apparently, these older aspen produce nutritionally superior buds and the branches are sturdier than those of other trees, allowing the ruffed grouse to feed with little flapping and balancing. Not only does precarious balancing require more energy to be expended, the very movement itself can serve as a flag to raptors, whose keen eyes are specially programmed to key in on movement.

Bump noted that not only are these branches well suited to support a ruffed grouse, the distribution of buds on the branches makes

These ironwood buds provide a lower quality food source for ruffed grouse than do those of the male aspen. Where aspen is unavailable, grouse will try to make do on ironwood, birch, hazel, or willow buds.

for efficient browsing. Normally there are 5 to 8 buds per twig, growing quite near each other. Thus, with a minimum of effort, a ruffed grouse can collect all of them. In less than 20 minutes of feeding it can consume 3 ounces of buds, which is a normal evening meal. This would be the equivalent of a 150-pound person consuming 27 pounds in a sitting.

Because the ruffed grouse stores very little fat, it must eat daily in the winter. Compare this to its neighbors. The black bear eats nothing all winter long because it is hibernating and burning stores of fat for energy, while the white-tailed deer actually eats less in the winter than in other months because it can slow its metabolism. The ruffed grouse lacks either winter adaptation, but fortunately for it, aspen buds are so high in proteins, fats, and sugars that the bird needs only feed about 15 to 20 minutes twice a day to supply itself with the necessary calories.

Most feedings occur just after sunrise and again at dusk. If the weather is extremely cold, ruffed grouse may skip the morning meal. Exposure to the subzero weather and winds would likely consume more

In areas where snowfall is rare or absent, ruffed grouse
frequently feed on the winter forest floor.

energy than the birds could ingest, which means that roosting beneath the snow for the morning may actually save energy. When they do go out to feed, they fly to the upper branches of these older aspen. It isn't unusual to see a small group of grouse feeding together in the same or adjacent trees. These are unrelated grouse of both sexes, and they likely gather because the choice trees border each bird's range. There may also be a safety mechanism involved, since ruffed grouse are very exposed to raptors while feeding. In this case, the more eyes the better, and of course, you only need to be faster than your neighbor if the group is attacked, thus increasing your odds of survival. These are the same predator avoidance strategies employed by herding animals such as elk and bison or flocks of grazing birds like geese.

When predator numbers are high, or when extremely cold weather dictates unusually long feeding periods, or when snow is insufficient for roosting, predation rates in winter can be quite high. Gullion noted that when these factors lead to losses of 65 to 70 percent of the fall's population, it will drive the grouse population below a level that the following year's reproduction can replace.

Fortunately, ruffed grouse populations are well able to withstand these mortality factors, for even if winter losses are severe for a winter or two, in the long run and with good habitat, ruffed grouse maintain their population. Come late winter, those ruffed grouse that survive the cold and the challenges of autumn are beginning to feel the hormonal urges to reproduce. As the snow melts, the cocks begin once again to strut, and the damp forest is alive with the sound of their drumming.

Winter may winnow the weak from the ranks of the ruffed grouse, but in the warmth of spring is the promise of renewal. And the ancient cycle repeats itself yet one more time.

All grouse, including this ruffed grouse, are adapted to cooler climates than are the species of the related pheasant family.

Overleaf: For the alert survivors of winter's challenges, the warmth of spring and a new reproductive cycle loom.

The Future of Ruffed Grouse

The world of the ruffed grouse is neither as simple nor as safe as we might have thought. Its relationship with the predators it feeds, and with the habitat that nurtures it, is complex and wonderful. Natural selection has seen to it that ruffed grouse have both the reproductive potential and the tools needed to survive nearly all forms of mortality. The one thing ruffed grouse can't do anything about, however, is the quality or quantity of habitat they have. Once, nature saw fit to balance these equations. Today, that role increasingly falls into the hands of humans.

In many ways, the ruffed grouse is a fortunate bird. There are many people who love this wary drummer in the woods, both for the pleasure of seeing or hearing it and for the experience of hunting and making it a meal. It is also fortunate that it depends upon a forest type that is not threatened. Birds and animals that require old forests are not nearly as lucky. Much of the ruffed grouse's life cycle is spent in young aspen forests.

The ruffed grouse, a handsome and exciting bird much valued by people, has a favorable future across much of its range.

Aspen is a tree species in high demand by the timber industry. It is also a tree species that regenerates quickly without expensive plantings, since clones grow from the roots and stumps of the trees cut down. These two factors mean that, on the whole, there's no large shortage of young aspen forests. However, it doesn't mean that aspen harvest can't be harmful to ruffed grouse. Large clearcuts, even in aspen forests, may leave ruffed grouse without the variety of habitat they need or the various age classes of trees they depend upon. Fortunately, public involvement in forestry issues in state and national forests has been successful in requiring that the industry modify its cutting patterns to benefit grouse and other wildlife. These same agencies, and advocacy groups like The Ruffed Grouse Society, also provide comprehensive literature or technical expertise to private landowners who wish to manage land in a manner beneficial to this bird.

Still, in parts of their range, especially in portions of the East, its habitat is less secure. Development and changing land use play big roles, for even the ruffed grouse can't exist in a suburban area. Though they can pioneer quickly into new habitat, they must have the specific requirements of nesting, brooding, and drumming cover. In the long run, how well ruffed grouse fare in the more heavily developed parts of their range depends largely upon how effectively we limit our sprawl and how wisely we use our forests.

Natural occurrences, even catastrophic failures due to poor weather conditions in winter, ill-timed cold, wet weather during the hatch, or the ups and downs of the grouse cycle, pose little threat to this resilient species. In fact, you might say they thrive on it, for it is exactly these conditions that shaped the ruffed grouse, that through the ages of natural selection purged the species of failures and built upon the genes of the strong.

The future of the ruffed grouse, then, is generally bright. It enjoys the attention and advocacy of hundreds of thousands of hunters, wildlife agencies, and others. Enlightened management of forests will, if we can keep our own population in check, ensure healthy habitats within which it can prosper.

If so, generations of us will be able to stroll through good grouse woods and enjoy as I did in my father's company so many years ago, the whirring dance of a grouse mother feigning injury. And we will continue to enjoy an autumn day behind the wagging tail of a fine bird dog.

Those are days both worth remembering, and worth working to ensure that they are repeated.

By considering the needs of ruffed grouse when planning logging, landowners and agencies help ensure the creation of good grouse habitat.

Further Reading

Managing Northern Forests for Wildlife, Gordon Gullion, 1984, The Ruffed Grouse Society.

Ruffed Grouse, S. Atwater and J. Schnell, editors, 1988, Stackpole Books.

Ruffed Grouse: Life History—Propagation—Management, Dr. Gardiner Bump, 1947, New York Conservation Department.

The Ruffed Grouse, Gordon Gullion, 1989, NorthWord Press, Inc.

Index